THE JESUS LIBRARY
edited by Michael Green

The Hard Sayings of Jesus
F. F. Bruce

The Teaching of Jesus
Norman Anderson

The Supremacy of Jesus
Stephen Neill

The Empty Cross of Jesus
Michael Green

The Counselling of Jesus
Duncan Buchanan

The Example of Jesus
Michael Griffiths

Jesus: Lord & Savior
F. F. Bruce

Other books by F. F. Bruce

The Books & the Parchments
The Defense of the Gospel in the New Testament
A History of the Bible in English
In Retrospect: Remembrance of Things Past
Israel & the Nations
Jesus & Christian Origins outside the New Testament
The Message of the New Testament
New Testament Development of Old Testament Themes
The New Testament Documents: Are They Reliable?
New Testament History
Paul & His Converts
Paul & Jesus
Peter, Stephen, James & John: Studies in Non-Pauline Christianity
The Spreading Flame
The Time Is Fulfilled

THE JESUS LIBRARY
Michael Green, series editor

Jesus: Lord & Savior

F. F. Bruce

INTERVARSITY PRESS
DOWNERS GROVE, ILLINOIS 60515

©1986 by F. F. Bruce

Published in the United States of America by InterVarsity Press, Downers Grove, Illinois, with permission from Hodder and Stoughton Limited, England.

InterVarsity Press is the book-publishing division of Inter-Varsity Christian Fellowship, a student movement active on campus at hundreds of universities, colleges and schools of nursing. For information about local and regional activities, write IVCF, 233 Langdon St., Madison, WI 53703.

Cover illustration: Janice Skivington

ISBN 0-87784-932-3
ISBN 0-87784-933-1 (The Jesus Library set)

Printed in the United States of America

Library of Congress Cataloging in Publication Data

Bruce, F. F., 1910-
    Jesus, Lord & Savior.

    (The Jesus library)
    Bibliography: p.
    Includes index.
    1. Jesus Christ—Person and offices.   I. Title.
II. Title: Jesus, Lord and Savior.   III. Series.
BT202.B765   1986   232   86-7157
ISBN 0-87784-932-3 (pbk.)

17   16   15   14   13   12   11   10   9   8   7   6   5   4   3   2
97   96   95   94   93   92   91   90   89   88   87

To
Louis and Olrunn Nielsen

Editor's Preface

It is a great pleasure to welcome a second contribution from Professor Bruce to The Jesus Library. His earlier book, *The Hard Sayings of Jesus*, has been widely appreciated in Britain and America, and I have no doubt that this volume will prove just as valuable.

Like the Athenians, the present generation has a tendency to be always seeking something new. Jesus is perceived as a freedom fighter, a guru, a magician, a drug user and a charlatan, according to the presuppositions of the literary or television writer. Minor finds, such as the lost letter of Clement of Alexandria about Mark (if it is genuine) are accorded major importance, and cause a short-lived furore in the popular press or on television. One of the many virtues of the present book is its great balance, based on encyclopaedic knowledge of the source material, the ancient background, and modern literature about the Gospels.

The result is not another 'Life of Jesus'. It is a careful study showing that the fashionable division between the Jesus of history and the Christ of faith is not tenable; and as well as taking us through who Jesus *was* Professor Bruce stresses who he *is* in the experience of believers – Son of God, Saviour, and Lord.

While other books in the series concentrate on some aspect of the life or teaching of Jesus, this is more of a general book to bring the central figure of the Christian faith into clear focus. It will give a great deal of information to Christians, and will be an ideal book to put in the hands of a thoughtful enquirer. It is an invaluable addition to The Jesus Library, and one for which I confidently predict a long future.

Michael Green

Author's Preface

With the completion of *The Hard Sayings of Jesus* I thought I had made my once-for-all contribution to the Jesus Library, but Michael Green's 'friendly and persuasive way', to which I referred in my preface to that volume, was brought to bear on me again – with the result that now lies before the reader.

Since the other titles in the series allocated to various authors deal with particular aspects of the person and work of our Lord, it seemed best that I should present a more general treatment, trying to answer the question 'Who is Jesus?' The present tense, 'Who *is* Jesus?' is chosen in preference to the past, 'Who *was* Jesus?' in order to emphasise that Jesus does not belong only to the first three decades of the Christian era, but is someone to be seriously and practically reckoned with today.

I have, as far as possible, avoided overlapping with *The Hard Sayings of Jesus* and also with another work (not included in the Jesus Library) entitled *Jesus and Christian Origins Outside the New Testament*. Where necessary, I have referred to these for fuller discussion of some matters touched upon in the present volume.

I shall be more than content if some of my readers find themselves confronted by the question which Jesus once put to his companions: 'Who do *you* say that I am?' If our answer is anything like so positive as theirs was, then it cannot remain an answer in words only.*

---

* Biblical quotations are generally from the Revised Standard Version, but I have frequently made my own translation where it seemed better suited to the context or the argument.

Introduction

Who is Jesus? The following pages give two answers to this question. First, he is a historical figure. Second, he is our eternal contemporary. Both these answers are true; both will be repeated in greater detail as we go on.

'Who is Jesus?' is a question that many people asked during the few years of his public activity early in the first century AD. The same question is debated with animation in many parts of the world today. Every now and then we are presented with a variety of answers to it in books or in television programmes. Some answers are supported by serious arguments; others are simply ventilated by way of novelty. One thing is clear: not all the answers can be right.

Here are some answers which we have been offered within the past twenty years: 'There never was such a person.' 'He was the founder of a drug-taking community which went in for religious hallucinations, and devised a code of lofty ethical teaching to provide a cover for its real activities.' 'He formed an inner group of disciples to whom he taught a libertine doctrine of freedom from moral restraint, while to the wider public he prescribed a high ethical standard.' 'He encouraged opposition to the occupying Roman forces in Judaea, making sure, for example, that his followers were armed at the last supper; the pacific teaching about turning the other cheek and so forth was ascribed to him at a later date, when his followers wished to distance themselves from the Jewish rebels whose revolt against Rome failed so disastrously in AD 70.' 'He was an Essene; his forty days in the wilderness were spent at the community headquarters of Khirbet Qumran, where he learned the doctrine taught by the Teacher of Righteousness – if indeed he was not himself the Teacher of Righteousness.' 'He had indeed some association with the Qumran community, but far from being the Teacher of Righteousness, he is denounced in the Qumran literature as the Wicked Priest, the implacable opponent of the Teacher of Righteousness.'

What these discordant answers have in common is that they all differ not merely from the New Testament witness to Jesus but from the account of him approved by the majority of modern historians within whose field his life and times fall.

It is not as though the wide range of speculation lying behind those answers were necessitated by the absence of hard evidence for more positive conclusions. The evidence is there, mainly in the pages of the New Testament. A generation ago one school of theologians kept on telling us that because the New Testament writers were preachers, not historians, the attempt to use their writings to discover the Jesus of history was both illegitimate and impossible. No one, we were assured, could write a life of Jesus, because the materials were not available. When this school was at the height of its influence, one scholar who defied them by doing what they pronounced to be impossible and illegitimate declared his conviction 'that a simple application of the normal standards of judgment with which historical and scientific study has made us familiar will enable us to arrive at a fair amount of accurate narrative'.[1]

This was a modest claim, and the scholar who made it justified it by taking over 200 pages to write his *Life of Jesus*. The evidence is not to be handled uncritically; we can, in fact, reach more certain and convincing conclusions when the accepted canons of historical study are fully utilised. But it is best not to be excessively influenced by one school of thought or climate of opinion. That was the trouble with the old, nineteenth-century 'quest of the historical Jesus' whose inadequacies were so thoroughly exposed by Albert Schweitzer in an epoch-making work.[2] The second half of the twentieth century has seen the rise of a 'new quest of the historical Jesus';[3] it remains to be seen if it will be more successful than its predecessor.

A nineteenth-century historian who was free from the influence of contemporary schools of theological thought and was, in fact, no believer in revealed religion, expressed this opinion about Jesus' abiding influence in an area of human life (ethics) which was to him one of special historical enquiry:

> The character of Jesus has not only been the highest pattern of virtue, but the strongest incentive to its practice, and has exerted so deep an influence, that it may be truly said, that the simple record of three short years of active life has done more to regenerate and to soften mankind, than all the disquisitions of philosophers and than all the exhortations of moralists.[4]

That is a non-Christian (or at least not distinctively Christian) judgment of one sense in which Jesus is not only a historical figure but also our eternal contemporary: his influence lives on. But there are other senses, as we shall see: Jesus himself lives on.[5]

Chapter
1

The Jesus of History and the Christ of Faith

'Disuniting' Jesus

There is a passage in the first letter of John, one of the later documents in the New Testament, where the writer warns his readers against accepting views about Jesus which undermine his true identity. Some of those views were put forth with the greater confidence because, it was claimed, they were taught by prophetic utterances which were prompted by the Spirit of God. John's reply to this claim is simple. There are many kinds of inspired utterance, he says, but not all of them are prompted by the Spirit of God; some of them proceed from quite a different kind of spirit. How then can it be known which inspired utterances are prompted by the Spirit of God and which are not? In this way, says John: what account do they give of Jesus Christ? If their testimony to him is in line with the gospel proclaimed by his first disciples, who received it directly from him, good and well. But if they teach something quite contrary to that gospel, then they are not to be listened to. The test to be applied to inspired utterances is the same as the test to be applied to all religious teaching. In John Newton's words:

> 'What think ye of Christ?' is the test
>   To try both your faith and your scheme;
> You cannot be right in the rest,
>   Unless you think rightly of him.

So, says John, 'every spirit which confesses that Jesus
Christ has come in the flesh is of God, and every spirit which
does not confess Jesus is not of God. This is the spirit of
antichrist' (1 John 4:2,3). The words, 'every spirit which does
not confess Jesus', mean (in the light of the words which
precede them) 'every spirit which does not confess that Jesus
Christ has come in the flesh'. But Ronald Knox's version of
the New Testament shows a somewhat different rendering:
'every spirit which acknowledges Jesus Christ as having come
to us in human flesh has God for its author; and no spirit which
would disunite Jesus comes from God.' His rendering of these
last words follows the wording of the Latin Bible, which
underlies Knox's translation. It is an attractive reading. The
main reason against accepting it is that it is so poorly attested
in the Greek manuscripts, the great majority of which read
'every spirit which does not confess Jesus' (or, more fully,
'every spirit which does not confess that Jesus Christ has come
in the flesh').

But what is meant by 'disuniting' Jesus? It probably means
disuniting the Jesus of history from the Christ of faith; it
refers, as Knox explains it in a footnote, to the teaching which
'would deny the identity of the human Jesus with the divine
Christ'. There was a school of thought in the later part of the
first century AD which regarded anything belonging to the
material order (including the human body) as religiously
worthless. The idea that God should reveal himself in a Jesus
of flesh and blood was unacceptable. Such a Jesus could be
dispensed with: the true Christ was a purely spiritual being. It
was to counter this line of argument that John, in his Gospel,
insisted that in Jesus of Nazareth the eternal Word or self-
expression of God 'became *flesh*' (John 1:14).

The peril of 'disuniting' Jesus in this way is with us still.
Listen to this, for example:

> The saving knowledge of God is not knowledge of and
> faith in Jesus, as a historic person portrayed in the Gospels.
> Christ is not to be equated with the historic Jesus. Christ is
> the Spirit of the Supreme, the Eternal Word. The mani-

festation of this Word in history is not limited to Jesus. Salvation is mediated through the Eternal Christ, the Word of God which is not to be confused with the historic Jesus.[1]

But these are the words not of a Christian but of a distinguished Indian philosopher, to whom the idea of the divine essence revealing itself through a succession of 'avatars' would be congenial. What is to be said, however, when a Christian theologian expresses himself as follows?

Jesus of Nazareth, the rabbi, the so-called historical Jesus, was an object of no interest for the early Christians, and is of no interest today for those who have preserved some understanding of what Christian faith means.[2]

In his later years that theologian might not have expressed himself so radically, but his general point of view was widely shared. It is the point of view represented by Rudolf Bultmann's forthright assertion that 'it is not the historical Jesus, but Jesus Christ the Preached One, who is the Lord'.[3]

To Professor Bultmann's forthright assertion, however, it should be said, with equal forthrightness, that it is both the historical Jesus *and* Jesus Christ the Preached One who is the Lord, because Jesus Christ the Preached One *is* the historical Jesus – one and the same Jesus, once crucified and now exalted. Any attempt to separate the two is apt to leave the Christ of faith, the Preached One, without a foundation, to make him the product of our faith instead of the ground of our faith, if not indeed to make him a figment of the imagination. The complaint has been voiced that too many who, in addresses to ecumenical assemblies and the like, invoke 'the mind of Christ' in relation to some contemporary issue do not think it necessary to bring the present mind of Christ into line with what can be known about the mind of the historical Jesus.[4] But if this is not done, what assurance can there be that the mind so confidently invoked is properly called the mind of Christ?

For example, if it be asked what the mind of Christ is about unfair racial discrimination, or a code of sexual ethics biased in favour of men, it is possible to give an answer because we have recorded utterances and attitudes of the historical Jesus to guide us. But on issues where no such guidance is available, especially on issues where Christians conscientiously differ, one should be cautious before saying positively what should be the Christian line, the application of the mind of Christ.

Revelation in history

If the Christian claim is well founded, that God revealed himself pre-eminently in the life and death of Jesus, then it is of the highest importance to know as completely and accurately as possible what kind of life and death it was in which God thus revealed himself. Christians of all people should be the last to play down the necessity of examining all the evidence that is available for the life and death of the historical Jesus. Happily, such evidence is readily accessible, inviting intelligent evaluation; and there is no reason for pessimism about the outcome of such evaluation.

Indeed, it is perfectly clear that no character in history excites more general interest, even today, than Jesus does. And in the first century, when people who had never seen him or heard him were urged to acknowledge him as Lord, they must inevitably have wanted to know as much as possible about the person to whom such a commitment was to be made. Jesus of Nazareth – his life, his activity, his teaching – must have been at least as interesting to them as he is to many people today.

Paul, the apostle to the Gentiles, made the death of Jesus so central to his preaching that it was as if 'Jesus Christ Crucified' had been placarded before his hearers' eyes. The first question they would ask was '*Why* was he crucified?' This demanded the recital of the whole of what is called the 'passion narrative' – not the death of Jesus only, but the events leading up to it: the mounting tension in Jerusalem during Jesus' last week, the authorities' decision to put him out of the way, Judas Iscariot's offer to help them to arrest him quietly, the actual arrest and the ensuing trial and condemnation.

The unknown author of the early Christian document called the letter to the Hebrews makes much of the help which the ascended Christ can give to his people when they pass through trials and temptations; but he emphasises that he is able to give this help the more effectively because, during his earthly life, he passed through the same trials and temptations himself.[5] The ministry which the ascended Christ continues to discharge for his people – what the author of Hebrews calls his ministry as their high priest in the presence of God – requires the continuity and identity of the earthly Jesus and the heavenly Christ. 'Jesus Christ is the same yesterday and today and forever' (Hebrews 13:8). Yesterday he was the historical Jesus; today he is the Christ of faith. But it is the identical Jesus Christ with whom we have to do, whether we think of him as he was in the early decades of the first century, or as he is in the closing decades of the twentieth century, or as he ever will be.

The Christ of faith, if disunited from the Jesus of history, is apt to be a figment of the pious imagination. The pious imagination, like any other kind of imagination, is an unsafe basis for faith and history alike. A good churchwoman, who must have been strangely sheltered from the facts of Christian history, was shocked one day to hear a preacher remark that Jesus was a Jew. She voiced her indignation to all who cared to listen to her: 'No, *sir*', she said; 'my Jesus was no Jew!' But the historical Jesus was indubitably a Jew, and if her Jesus was no Jew, then her Jesus was not the Jesus of history, and in some degree at least was a figment of her pious imagination. More culpable by far was the dictum of the Minister for Propaganda and Public Enlightenment of the German Reich in Hitler's administration: 'Jesus was not a Jew. Historical proof is not necessary; it is so.' Neither piety nor imagination was at work there, but anti-Jewish prejudice. It mattered nothing to Dr Goebbels what Jesus' nationality was, or whether he had any nationality at all; his concern was to persuade people to believe something in line with his government's philosophy.

We must begin, then, with the historical Jesus, a real man of flesh and blood, who lived his life of something over thirty years at a particular time and place – in the first few decades of the Christian era and in the land of Israel. We must consider the nature of the available evidence for his life and teaching, and then see what can be said of him in the light of that evidence. The church's time-honoured creeds, in which the doctrine of the person of Christ was later formulated, cannot take the place of historical evidence; their credibility depends on their consistency with what can be known of the historical Jesus. Nearly a hundred years ago, in an earlier phase of the modern debate about the person of Christ, a wise man wrote, 'Councils, we admit, and Creeds, cannot go behind, but must wholly rest upon the history of our Lord Jesus Christ.'[6] That remains true; only, we do not merely 'admit' it, we assert it. So, to the history of our Lord Jesus Christ let us go.

Chapter
2

Jesus—the Evidence

The New Testament documents

In my younger days there were two books by a Cambridge
scholar, T. R. Glover, which enjoyed wide influence in many
parts of the world: *The Jesus of History* (1917) and *Jesus in the
Experience of Men* (1921). The former was the more influential in its time; the latter, I think, was the better book. But the
titles of these two books indicate two lines along which
evidence for Jesus can be sought. We can view him in his
historical setting; we can consider the impact he has made on
human life from the first century to the twentieth. One minor
impact he has made is indicated by our speaking of the first
century and the twentieth. This way of reckoning time is in
worldwide use, among Christians and non-Christians alike,
because his coming into the world marked a new beginning
for the human race.[1]

Here, however, we are concerned with the evidence for the
historical Jesus. Our primary evidence for him lies in the New
Testament documents. It is interesting to study the earliest
references to him in non-Christian literature, but these are
few and unimportant, and need not engage our attention
here.[2] As for the New Testament documents, it is foolish to
regard their evidence as suspect because they were produced
within the society which confessed Jesus as Lord. It is more
likely that the memoirs of any great leader will be recorded
and preserved among his followers than among those who
have no sympathy with him. Practically all we know about

Socrates comes from Plato and Xenophon, two very different men who had sat at his feet. When we try to reconstruct the historical Socrates, we do not ignore the testimony of Plato and Xenophon because they were his disciples; we take account of that fact, and we also take account of the two men's very different capacities for understanding the master's teaching and drawing out its implications. Another contemporary picture of Socrates, this time from outside the circle of his disciples, is given by Aristophanes in his comedy *The Clouds*: it probably represents what the man in the Athenian street thought of Socrates – a crackpot, not to say a charlatan – and is self-evidently a caricature.

The earliest New Testament writings are the earlier letters of Paul. Paul never knew the historical Jesus, but he knew men who had been closely associated with him. About five years after the death of Jesus, Paul spent two weeks in Jerusalem with Peter, the most prominent figure among Jesus' disciples, and met James, the brother of Jesus (Galatians 1:18,19). Paul wrote no Gospel, as the evangelists did, but in his letters he could draw where necessary on his knowledge of what Jesus had done and said. In particular, he reminds his converts more than once that in his first instruction of them he 'delivered' to them something that he himself had 'received' – received, that is to say, at the beginning of his Christian career. The two verbs he uses denote the handing down of tradition, and his language points to the way in which the gospel and the teaching of Jesus were transmitted orally before they were first written down.

The four Gospels

We are fortunate in having, in the four Gospels in the New Testament, documents which have probably been subjected, over the past two centuries, to more sustained critical analysis than any comparable body of literature in the world.

They may be assessed from the viewpoint of historical

criticism. They can be related to all that is known about the position of Palestine in the Roman world in the early decades of the first Christian century. Since Jesus and all the main figures in the gospel story were Jews, what we are told about them can be related to what is known about the Jews, and especially Palestinian Judaism, in that period.[3]

The literary criticism of the Gospels is a fascinating study largely stimulated by the fact that there are four of them, with much material that is common to two or more. In particular, the Gospels of Matthew, Mark and Luke have so much material in common that their contents can be arranged in three parallel columns, where one can see at a glance what is common to two or three and what is peculiar to one. It is because they lend themselves to this 'synoptic' presentation that these three are called the synoptic Gospels. The conclusion usually (and I think rightly) drawn from their comparative study is that the Gospel of Mark (or something very like it) served as a source for the Gospels of Matthew and Luke, and that these two also had access to a collection of sayings of Jesus (conventionally labelled 'Q'), which may have been compiled as a handbook for the Gentile mission around AD 50. And these by no means exhaust the sources of information, written or oral, which were at the evangelists' disposal.

Two other forms of criticism which have a place in the study of the Gospels are tradition criticism and redaction criticism. Tradition here refers to the gospel material which the evangelists received; redaction refers to their treatment of that material. For they were not mechanical scissors-and-paste operators; they were responsible authors, each with his own perspective and aim. Tradition criticism tries to trace the transmission of the material in the oral stage, before it acquired the form given to it by the evangelists or their predecessors; redaction criticism pays attention to the form in which they individually presented it.

All these lines of critical study have their place: some are more fruitful than others. But what we have confronting us today is the fourfold gospel. What then, when criticism has done its perfect work, can be said about the individual documents which make it up?[4]

Mark probably wrote his Gospel in the first instance for the Christians of Rome in the aftermath of the persecution which overtook them without warning under Nero, as a sequel to the great fire in July, AD 64. In their bewilderment and disorientation they needed to be reassured about their identity. This little book, containing the Christian society's own account of the events which gave it birth and in particular of the ministry and passion of its founder, 'had the character of a call to Christian loyalty and a challenge to a hostile world'.[5] It reminded them that to suffer for Christ's sake was not something strange or unnatural, but something rather to be expected. Jesus had not only insisted repeatedly on the necessity for his own suffering, but also on the certainty that those who were determined to follow him would have to 'take up the cross' after him.

As for the two other synoptic Gospels, Matthew has the character of a well arranged manual for the use of teachers; its distinctive feature is the fivefold body of discourse material in which it collects the teaching of Jesus.[6] At the end of this Gospel Jesus instructs the apostles to go and 'make disciples of all nations', teaching their converts to cherish and practise all that they themselves had learned from him (Matthew 28:19,20). Christian teachers of a later generation who took up the torch from the apostles would have found in Matthew's Gospel a handbook admirably designed to help them in their task. Luke, for his part, compiled a history of Christian origins in two volumes (the second volume being known to us as the Acts of the Apostles) at a time when Christianity was coming increasingly to the attention of people in places of responsibility in the Roman world. There were many garbled accounts of Christianity in circulation; Luke aimed to provide a reliable and orderly account of its rise and progress.

The Gospel of John, to be dated later in the first century AD, has a much larger element of theological interpretation than the other Gospels. Theological interpretation is not indeed lacking in them: Mark, in particular, insists that Jesus is the Son of God. So does John, but his special contribution to the gospel witness is his presentation of Jesus as 'the Word made flesh' – in him, that is to say, the eternal wisdom of God became incarnate in a human life.[7] This is the teaching of his prologue (John 1:1–18), and he intends the rest of his Gospel to be understood in the light of this. But it is a Gospel, not a theological treatise, that he writes; his theological interpretation is constructed on a historical framework, independent of the historical framework that the synoptic evangelists have in common. Whereas in the synoptic record most of Jesus' ministry is located in Galilee, John places most of it in Jerusalem and its neighbourhood. But in John, as in the synoptic record, the ministry begins in the setting of John the Baptist's mission in the Jordan valley and ends with Jesus' death in Jerusalem, while its crucial mid-point is marked by a confession volunteered by Peter soon after the feeding of the five thousand (the one 'miracle' reported by all four evangelists).

The points of coincidence between the Johannine narrative framework and that of the other Gospels provide an opportunity to apply one of the 'criteria of authenticity'. These criteria are a series of tests to which the gospel material is subjected by some students in an attempt to establish that Jesus really did speak and act in the ways variously indicated by the evangelists. Some of them are of only limited usefulness. The criterion of *dissimilarity* assigns relatively high credibility to those sayings or actions of Jesus which are unparalleled either in Judaism or in early Christianity. But, since Jesus was a Jew, we should expect to find many contacts with Judaism in his life and teaching; and since the early Christians looked to him as their teacher and exemplar *par excellence*, it is natural that they should have perpetuated many features for which he provided the precedent. The criterion of *coherence* attaches high probability to sayings or actions which are consistent with others whose credibility is established by the criterion of dissimilarity. The criterion with which we are concerned at present is the criterion of *multiple attestation*: when the same saying or action of Jesus is recorded independently by two or more gospel sources, or by the Gospels of Mark and John, then the likelihood of its being historically genuine is proportionately increased. But here again: the genuineness of a saying or action ascribed to him is not to be discounted or treated as suspect merely because it is found in one source, or in one Gospel, only.

The outline of Jesus' ministry and the main thrust of his teaching can be derived with substantial confidence from the evidence of the four Gospels.

Recent discoveries

It may be asked if recent discoveries – say within the past half-century – have helped to solve some problems of gospel study. Two bodies of literature came to light in the 1940s, to which some have looked in expectation of such help. One is the material from the Qumran library in the wilderness of Judaea (commonly called the Dead Sea Scrolls); the other is the collection of papyrus codices from the neighbourhood of Nag Hammadi in Upper Egypt. Neither of these throws direct light on the Gospels. I have dealt with them more fully elsewhere,[8] so a brief indication of their relevance will be sufficient here.

The Qumran texts supply information about a community of Jews, evidently an Essene group, which withdrew from the main stream of national life and established itself in the wilderness for about two centuries (approximately 130 BC–AD 70), preparing for the new age which (it was believed) God was about to inaugurate. Most of the texts thus far published must be dated before the birth of Jesus, and therefore can make no reference to him; but the knowledge gathered from them about one phase of Jewish faith and religious practice provides us with welcome background material for our study of the Gospels and other New Testament writings.

The Nag Hammadi finds comprise fifty-two Coptic documents bound in thirteen papyrus codices, which evidently belonged to the library of a Christian community in Upper Egypt in the fourth century AD. Most of them are translations of earlier Greek documents, which in their original language are almost without exception lost. They present interpretations of Christianity (usually categorised as 'Gnostic') which are characteristic of the second century and later rather than the first. Only one of them preserves any direct contact with the historical Jesus: that is the 'Gospel of Thomas', a collection of 114 sayings ascribed to Jesus. About half of these have parallels in the canonical Gospels. Others are sufficiently similar to them to satisfy the 'criterion of coherence'; there are some, however, which reflect interests different from those of first-century Palestine.

In addition to major finds like those at Qumran and Nag Hammadi, every now and then some isolated document, or part of a document, turns up which promises to have some bearing on the gospel story.

Fifty years ago, for example, the British Museum published a volume with the title *Fragments of an Unknown Gospel*, which presented the text of some pieces of papyrus which had recently been found in Egypt.[9] These fragments, however, did not really come from a new Gospel; they exhibited some words and actions of Jesus (a dispute with lawyers, the healing of a leper, the incident of the tribute money, and an apocryphal account of Jesus' sowing seed on the Jordan) based mainly on the canonical Gospels and in part on an uncanonical Gospel. The work to which they belonged was probably a popular re-telling of the ministry of Jesus.

In 1958 Professor Morton Smith of New York found in the library of the Mar Saba monastery, twelve miles south-east of Jerusalem, a copy of a book printed in Amsterdam in 1646, on the end-papers of which someone had written in Greek part of a letter purporting to be the work of Clement of Alexandria, who flourished around AD 180. Whoever wrote this text on the end-papers had presumably copied it from a manuscript which can no longer be located. It may well be that the text belongs to a genuine letter of Clement, though this is disputed by some. However, its main interest lies in the reference it makes to a longer edition of the Gospel of Mark, which the evangelist is said to have provided for 'advanced' believers in Alexandria. It reproduces after Mark 10:34 the story of Jesus raising a rich young man from the tomb and teaching him in the course of one night 'the mystery of the kingdom of God'. The story has affinities with the raising of Lazarus in John 11 and also with the account in John 3:1–15 of Nicodemus's visit to Jesus 'by night' and learning from him the conditions for entry to the kingdom of God.[10]

Interesting as such minor discoveries always are, it must be confessed that they add little or nothing in the way of evidence to what we already know.

Chapter
3

Jesus—the Historical Setting

The background

'Jesus was born in Bethlehem of Judea in the days of Herod the king', says Matthew the evangelist (Matthew 2:1), thus indicating the place and time of Jesus' birth. Only two of the New Testament writers give us any details of the birth of Jesus: Matthew is one, and Luke is the other. Both of them say that he was born in Bethlehem, although they know (in common with the other evangelists) that Jesus was brought up in Nazareth, a town in Galilee, and was called 'Jesus of Nazareth'. But Matthew and Luke are independent of each other in their birth narratives. Matthew connects Jesus' birth in Bethlehem with an Old Testament oracle predicting that the ruler of Israel would come from there, as King David had come over a thousand years before (Micah 5:2). Luke, for his part, explains that at that time a census was being held which required each householder or head of a family to be registered at the place to which his family belonged, and Joseph for that reason had to go and register at Bethlehem. He took his wife Mary with him, and while they were in Bethlehem her firstborn child, Jesus, was born.

Luke also implies that Jesus was born in the reign of Herod; at least he introduces his account of the conception and birth of John the Baptist (who, he says, was six months older than Jesus) with the words, 'In the days of Herod, king of Judea' (Luke 1:5).

If Jesus was born in the reign of Herod, it must have been

right at the end of his reign. Herod ruled as king of the Jews
from 37 to 4 BC, and Luke says later on that in the fifteenth
year of the Emperor Tiberius – meaning probably the year
AD 27–28 – Jesus 'was about thirty years of age' (Luke
3:1,23). But who was this Herod, and how did he become king
of the Jews?

The Jews once had a native dynasty of kings, founded by
David before 1000 BC. It lasted for over 400 years, but then it
was brought to an end by the Babylonians, who incorporated
Judaea into their empire and deported many of its inhabitants
(587 BC). But a couple of generations later the Babylonians
were defeated by the Persians under Cyrus. Cyrus, being a
statesman as well as a military genius, realised the wisdom of
allowing displaced persons here and there throughout his
empire to return home, if they so wished. Several thousand
Jewish exiles went back to Judaea, where they rebuilt their
temple in Jerusalem and enjoyed religious freedom. There
was no question of granting them political independence;
they remained under Persian control for just over 200 years,
when the Persian Empire was overthrown in its turn by
Alexander the Great, at the head of an army of Macedonians
and Greeks. Judaea fell into Alexander's hands in 332 BC and
was governed by him and his successors for 190 years. During
those years the Jews flourished, not only in Judaea but in
other parts of the Graeco-Macedonian Empire – notably in
the great Egyptian city of Alexandria, founded by Alexander
and named after himself in 331 BC. They enjoyed the ameni-
ties of Greek civilisation, and continued to practise their
ancestral worship without hindrance.

The day came, however, when one of Alexander's successors, Antiochus IV, commonly called Antiochus Epiphanes,
decided to abolish the Jews' ancestral worship, or at least to
assimilate it so thoroughly to a Greek cult that it would lose its
distinctiveness. His chief motive was the safeguarding of the
security of his kingdom; he was wrongly persuaded by unwise
advisers that his action against the Jewish religion would
strengthen his position in face of external dangers. For three
years (167–164 BC) the Jerusalem temple was given over to

the worship of a Greek divinity, stigmatised by the Jews as 'the abomination of desolation'. The Jews had been docile subjects of their Persian and Graeco-Macedonian overlords so long as their religious freedom was unimpaired, but the action of Antiochus stirred up a spirit of resentment which found an outlet in armed rebellion. Judas Maccabaeus, a gifted guerrilla leader, won a succession of victories against armies much larger and better equipped than his own following, and at the end of 164 BC was able to regain religious freedom for his people and restore the temple to its proper purpose. The anniversary of the dedication of the purified temple became a national festival among the Jews: it is mentioned in John 10:22, where Jesus is said to have been at 'the feast of the Dedication at Jerusalem' during the last winter of his life.

Many pious Jews would have been content with the regaining of religious freedom, but Judas Maccabaeus and his brothers continued their campaign in hope of securing political independence. This hope was realised in 142 BC, when Judaea became an independent state under Simon, the last survivor of Judas's brothers. Simon, followed by his heirs and successors, was not only civil and military leader but high priest as well. He and his family – the Hasmonaean family – were of priestly descent, but did not belong to the house of Zadok, which had held the chief-priestly office in Jerusalem (apart from the interruption caused by the Babylonian exile) from the time that Solomon built the first temple there until Antiochus IV deposed the last Zadokite high priest – a period of 800 years.

Various aspects of the Hasmonaean dynasty's policy, and especially its assumption of the high-priesthood, incurred the disapproval of pious groups among the Jews. One group found their rule so intolerable that it withdrew from public life and settled in the Judaean wilderness at Qumran (and possibly other centres). This group belonged to the nonconformist tradition of the Essenes.[1] Another group, the party of the Pharisees, did not withdraw from public life but remained as the predominant opposition to the Hasmonaeans for most of the time that they were in power.[2] Over against them, the Hasmonaeans enjoyed the support of another party, called the Sadducees.[3]

The Hasmonaeans ruled an independent Judaea for nearly eighty years, from 142 to 63 BC. During those years the power of the Romans was steadily increasing in Western Asia. Judaea would soon have become subservient to the Romans in any case, but an opportunity was given to them to establish their power there when a quarrel broke out between two Hasmonaean princes and one of them invited the Romans to intervene on his side. The Roman occupation of Judaea in 63 BC brought Hasmonaean sovereignty to an end.

Judaea proved a difficult province for the Romans to administer, and at last they decided to rule it through a Jewish king, Herod by name, a member of an influential family which had recently made itself very useful to Rome. Herod was not a popular ruler: he did not belong to any of the royal families of Israel, whether Davidic or Hasmonaean, being in fact the descendant of Edomites (Idumaeans) who had been forcibly converted to Judaism a few generations earlier. But he ruled his kingdom effectively in Rome's interests for thirty-three years. In his will he divided his kingdom among three of his sons, but his will had to be confirmed by Augustus, the Roman emperor, before it could take effect. One son (Archelaus) became ruler of Judaea and Samaria, another (Herod Antipas) was given Galilee and Peraea (Transjordan), and a third (Philip) inherited territory east and north of the lake of Galilee, where he built a new capital for himself at Caesarea Philippi, near one of the sources of the Jordan.

All three of these sons of Herod are mentioned in the Gospels.[4] Two of them – Herod Antipas and Philip – were still governing their tetrarchies during the ministry of Jesus, thirty years and more after they were installed in office. But Archelaus proved to be so oppressive a ruler that after nine years his subjects petitioned Augustus to remove him and govern Judaea directly through a lieutenant of his own. In AD 6, then, Judaea became a Roman province, administered on the emperor's behalf by an official first called a prefect and later a procurator.

The Jews of Palestine in Jesus' day

While Jesus was born in Bethlehem, he spent his boyhood and youth in Nazareth. In this Galilaean town he was brought up, with four brothers and an unspecified number of sisters, in the house of Joseph, the local carpenter or builder. Joseph appears to have died before Jesus emerged into public view; his wife Mary, Jesus' mother, lived on to become, with the rest of her family, a founding member of the primitive church in Jerusalem.[5] It was no secret that the family could trace its ancestry back to King David; Jesus himself, however, laid no weight on this, although he did not repudiate the designation 'son of David' when others gave it to him.

When Judaea became a Roman province, the prefect chose Caesarea, on the Mediterranean seaboard, as his seat of government; it was a largely Gentile city and, for a Roman, a much more congenial place to reside in than Jerusalem. But in the eyes of Jews Jerusalem remained the capital; it was indeed the religious centre of Jewish life no matter how widely dispersed throughout the world the Jews might be. Here stood the temple, God's one visible dwelling-place on earth. King Herod had completely rebuilt it and made it one of the most magnificent structures of its time. Here and here alone the Jewish priesthood functioned, offering up sacrifices to the God of Israel day by day and year by year. The head of all the Jewish priests was the high priest. Between AD 6 and 41 the high priest owed his appointment to the Roman governor, so this department of national life was as firmly under the control of Rome as all others.

In addition to his sacred functions, the high priest for the time being was also president of the Sanhedrin, the supreme court of the Jewish nation, which retained control of internal affairs, although it was ultimately answerable to the Roman governor. It comprised seventy elders in addition to the high priest. The majority of these elders belonged to the wealthy party of the Sadducees. The aristocratic families from which the high priest and leading temple officials were regularly drawn at this period were Sadducees. The Pharisees formed the minority group in the Sanhedrin, but their standing among the people was such that they exercised an influence out of proportion to their numbers.

The Sadducees do not figure significantly in the record of Jesus' ministry. With the Pharisees, on the other hand, he was involved in controversy almost from the beginning of his public activity. The Pharisees, in reaction against prevalent laxity, were concerned about the scrupulous observance of the Jewish law. They banded themselves together in local brotherhoods to encourage one another in its study and practice. Their number was reckoned to amount to about 6,000 at this time. Many people who were not themselves members of their party followed their direction. Most of the 'scribes', the professional students and teachers of the scriptures, belonged to one or another of the Pharisaic schools and popularised their teaching. But not all scribes were Pharisees; there were others who expounded the law in accordance with Sadducean tenets, ignoring 'the tradition of the elders'.[6]

The 'tradition of the elders' was largely designed to adapt the ancient written law to the conditions of a day far removed from that in which it had originally been given. If, for example, the fourth commandment forbade the doing of any 'work' on the sabbath day, it was necessary to define what was work and what was not in the Palestinian situation of the first century AD. The accumulated body of adaptation and interpretation, which was transmitted by word of mouth, came to be regarded as a law-code in itself, the oral law over against the written law, and in theory at least it was held to go back to Moses, who (it was affirmed) received it from God on Mount Sinai along with the written law.

The Pharisees' meticulous observance of the laws of levitical purity made it difficult for them to associate too closely – at table, for example – with their fellow-Jews who were not so particular about such matters. They also took very seriously the practice of tithing – donating ten per cent of all income and produce to the service of God – to the point where they tithed not only major crops like barley and wheat, grapes and olives, but also garden herbs. Their unwillingness to eat anything of the sort unless they could be sure that the tithe had been properly paid on it constituted a further barrier to sharing meals with other Jews. Here was one marked difference between Jesus' life-style and theirs, for he was notoriously ready to enjoy table-fellowship with people who had no foothold in respectable society.

Political issues

During Jesus' ministry the high priest in Jerusalem was Joseph, surnamed Caiaphas. He was appointed to the office in AD 18 by Valerius Gratus, prefect of Judaea, and held it for eighteen years. When Pontius Pilate succeeded Valerius Gratus as prefect in AD 26, he left Caiaphas in occupation of the high priesthood; probably he was given reason to think that it would be more to his advantage to leave Caiaphas in office than to replace him by someone else. Both he and Caiaphas were removed from their respective offices in AD 36 by Lucius Vitellius, Roman governor of Syria, under whose authority the prefect of Judaea was.

Caiaphas was a member (by marriage) of the most powerful of all the high-priestly families in the New Testament era. He was son-in-law to Annas, who had been high priest from AD 6 to 15. When Annas was removed from office, he remained the power behind the high-priestly throne for many years. Five of his sons and one grandson (in addition to his son-in-law Caiaphas) occupied the high-priesthood at various times between AD 16 and 68.

It was only in Jerusalem that Jesus came into contact with the high priest or the Roman prefect, and that in the closing days of his life. In Galilee he lived under the rule of the tetrarch Herod Antipas. Antipas was an astute statesman – it was not for nothing that Jesus once referred to him as 'that fox' (Luke 13:32). He knew that he owed his principality to the grace of the Roman emperor, and he made it his business to maintain the emperor's goodwill. Not once did he put a foot wrong until, in old age, he allowed his wife Herodias to persuade him against his instinct and better judgment to take action which resulted in his deposition and exile. The emperor expected him to preserve law and order in his tetrarchy, and he acted swiftly against anyone who seemed likely to become a focus of disaffection. John the Baptist suffered imprisonment and death on this account, and later the tetrarch's suspicions were directed against Jesus. But for one who lived beside the lake of Galilee, as Jesus did during the greater part of his ministry, it was easy to escape Antipas's attention by taking a ship to the other side, to the territory of his brother Philip, where there were no such tensions as troubled both Galilee and Judaea.

About four miles north of Nazareth lay Sepphoris, where Antipas had his residence until about AD 22. He then moved from there to a new capital which he built for himself at Tiberias on the lakeside and named in honour of the Emperor Tiberius. Reports of happenings at the tetrarch's court would quickly be carried to Nazareth and other neighbouring towns. Historic scenes of Israel's ancient history were within view of the hilltop overlooking Nazareth, and just as familiar to one who lived there were the realities of the nation's present plight.

Nazareth might be a place of no great repute, a backwater, off the beaten track; but its inhabitants were not insulated from current events. When the holy family returned there during Jesus' infancy, they would be told the full story of the troubles which had afflicted Galilee immediately after the death of Herod. The chief of those troubles was a rising led by a man named Judas, who with a band of fellow-insurgents raided the royal palace at Sepphoris and seized the contents of the armoury. Thus equipped for military action, they dominated the region and were not put down until Quinctilius Varus, Roman governor of Syria, marched south with two legions to crush the revolt and pacify the land. The Roman idea of pacification was demonstrated by Varus's crucifixion of two thousand ringleaders of the revolt: their bodies remained fastened to the crosses along the main roads for a long time, as a deterrent to others.[7]

Nine years later, when Judaea to the south was made a Roman province after the deposition of Archelaus, news arrived at Nazareth and elsewhere of a rising led by another Judas in protest against the new order in Judaea.[8] This rising was crushed in its turn, but its ideals lived on in what Josephus calls the 'fourth philosophy' – the doctrine, that is to say, that it was impermissible for the people of God, living in the land which he gave them, to hand over the produce of that land by way of tribute to a Gentile ruler. For, now that Judaea was an imperial province, its inhabitants were required to pay taxes to the emperor; indeed, the new governor of Syria, Quirinius, held a census to determine the amount of taxation to be levied from Judaea for the imperial exchequer. The people of Galilee, although they were not directly involved in this rising, would be the more keenly interested in it because its leader, Judas, belonged to the territory just across the lake of Galilee. No one, even in the remotest parts of Galilee, could forget the problems and conflicts raised by the Roman presence. The hope of liberation burned in the hearts of many, whether it was expected to come through divine intervention or by armed struggle. When Jesus launched his Galilaean ministry by proclaiming release for the captives and liberation for the oppressed, he had to make it crystal clear that his proclamation was not to be realised by military or political means; and many of his hearers were slow to believe that he meant what he said. Even so, when he left the relative security of Galilee and ventured into the area of direct Roman rule, it was at the hands of the Roman power that he met his death.

Chapter
4

The Beginning of Jesus' Ministry

The Ministry of John the Baptist

All four evangelists place Jesus' first public appearance in the context of the ministry of John the Baptist.

John was a preacher of repentance whose short-lived but memorable activity began in the wilderness of Judaea about AD 27. Many of his hearers believed that in him the voice of prophecy, unheard in Israel for generations, had once again sounded forth: the common people 'all held that John was a real prophet' (Mark 11:32). It was no general call for repentance that he uttered: divine judgment was about to be exercised, he proclaimed, and the one to whom the judgment was entrusted was shortly to be manifested. 'His winnowing fork is in his hand, to clear his threshing floor, and to gather the wheat into his granary, but the chaff he will burn with unquenchable fire' (Luke 3:17). Whereas John himself baptised people in water, this coming one would baptise them with the Holy Spirit. The Holy Spirit would prove to be a spirit of judgment: as the wind blew the chaff away from the threshing-floor and the fire burned it up, so the baptism to be administered by the coming one would be a baptism of wind and fire. It was in view of this imminent judgment that John called his fellow-Israelites to repent and to seal their repentance by receiving baptism at his hands in the Jordan.

It was in these circumstances that Jesus came to the place where John was preaching, and persuaded him to baptise him too. Jesus wished to associate himself publicly with what he

recognised to be the work of God; in the light of his subsequent ministry we can see symbolic significance in his
determination at this early stage to identify himself with
sinners (for those who came to John for baptism confessed
that they were sinners). To Jesus, his baptism was his dedication to do the will of God, and the divine call to his life-
mission came to him as he came up out of the Jordan. It came
to him in the form of a voice from heaven: 'You are my Son,
my beloved one; in you I delight' (Mark 1:11). The Old
Testament background of these words gave them meaning:
Jesus, they indicated, was the long-expected Messiah, the
Lord's anointed, but he was to fulfil his messianic destiny
along the path marked out for the Servant of the Lord who is
introduced in Isaiah 42:1 – a path of self-effacement and
suffering. Jesus' acceptance of this calling was put to the test
in the immediately ensuing temptations in the wilderness:
these attempts were in essence suggestions that he might fulfil
his messianic destiny along other paths than that which he
now knew to be the way of God's will for him.

John the Baptist's reaction to Jesus' baptism was to recognise him as the coming one of whom he had spoken – the
stronger one than himself who was to baptise people with the
Spirit. He experienced some bewilderment a little later when
reports of Jesus' activity made no reference to the work of
judgment that he had forecast for the coming one.

John's ministry was not confined to the wilderness of
Judaea or the banks of the Jordan. The fourth Gospel speaks
of his baptising people in Samaria – probably in the well-
watered region around the confluence of the Wadi Baida and
the Wadi Fara'a. But it was in the territory of Herod Antipas
that a sudden end was put to his public activity. He denounced
Antipas's marriage to his sister-in-law and niece Herodias in
terms which moved Antipas to arrest him and imprison him in
his Transjordanian fortress of Machaerus. There, not long
afterwards, he was put to death.

Jesus' proclamation of the kingdom of God

During the later phase of John's ministry Jesus pursued a concurrent ministry in Judaea, but the news of John's imprisonment sent him north to Galilee (although that was the major area of Herod Antipas's tetrarchy); and there, in the towns and villages west of the lake, he embarked on a new and systematic ministry – the preaching of the kingdom of God. The background to his use of this term is to be found in the book of Daniel, where it is announced that the time will come when 'the God of heaven will set up a kingdom which shall never be destroyed' (Daniel 2:44) – a kingdom which is to supersede all earthly kingdoms. Without further explanation, such a proclamation would certainly have been taken to mean that the day of Israel's liberation was at hand, when the Roman Empire and minor Gentile powers would disappear. This was not what Jesus meant when he affirmed that the kingdom of God had drawn near; what he did mean was made clear in his teaching and in his actions.

The kingdom of God took its character in Jesus' teaching chiefly from the nature of the God whose kingdom it was. Jesus spoke of God as Father. He was not unique in this, but the word that he used was Abba, the word used by children in the family circle when they addressed their father or talked about him. It was another, rather more formal, term that was used when God was addressed as Father in synagogue prayers. Jesus taught his followers to call God by this familiar term, and to look to him with the same trustful expectancy that children at home show towards their father. There was something so distinctive about Jesus' use of the form Abba that in the next generation it found its way into the religious vocabulary of the church – not only the primitive Aramaic-speaking church (which was natural, since Abba is an Aramaic word) but the wider Greek-speaking church as well. When Christians call 'Abba! Father!' they show, according to Paul, that they are indwelt by the same Spirit as animated Jesus (Galatians 4:6).

The special prayer which Jesus taught his disciples opens

with this intimate word: 'Father, may your name be sanctified' (Luke 11:2). The prayer itself summarises his teaching about God. God is the Father who supplies his children's material needs and spiritual needs alike. They are encouraged to pray, almost in the same breath, for the accomplishment of his eternal purpose in the world (the coming of his kingdom), for their daily bread, for the forgiveness of their sins and for deliverance in times when their faith in him is tested to the limit.

The kingdom of God, in Jesus' preaching, is not imposed by force; it is the new order in which men and women freely accept God's will as their way of life, forgiving one another as he has forgiven them, giving service rather than demanding it.

Jesus taught his hearers about the kingdom of God in straight instruction and by means of parables. The parable might be the story of some action or situation which would win their spontaneous assent, until they began to reflect on the implications of their assent. Or it might tell of some action so much at variance with everyday practice that they would be shaken out of the complacency of their assumptions and be forced to think about some aspect of their relation to one another, or to God.

Some of the parables spoke of the nature of the kingdom of God. It was like seed that was sown broadcast: much depended on the kind of ground on which it was sown. When it fell into the right kind of soil where it could germinate and begin to grow, its growth was unseen for some time, but something was nevertheless at work beneath the surface. A small and insignificant amount of leaven might be put into a large quantity of flour, but when once it began to work it would continue until the whole batch of dough had risen. There was no comparison between the tiny mustard-seed and the large plant which was propagated from it: similarly there was no comparison between the present modest beginnings of the kingdom of God and what it would yet become. Just as a merchant would sell his whole stock in order to buy something that surpassed it all in value, so men and women with any appreciation of the kingdom of God would gladly let everything else go for the sake of gaining this 'pearl of great price' (Matthew 13:46 KJV).

Jesus' teaching ministry was accompanied by a healing ministry. News of his power to cure bodily and mental diseases by a word or a touch spread rapidly abroad, and he was beset by people coming to him from all the surrounding region, and even from further afield, who sought healing for themselves or their friends. By this ministry of mercy and power, as well as by the spoken word, Jesus made known something of the nature of the kingdom of God: the relieving of those who were demon-possessed, in particular, was a sign, as he said, that 'the kingdom of God has come upon you' (Luke 11:20).

Good news for the poor

When John the Baptist, now imprisoned by Herod Antipas, heard from some of his disciples what Jesus was doing, he found it difficult to reconcile with the programme of judgment that he had predicted for the coming one, so he sent two of them to Jesus with the question: 'Are you the coming one, or must we look for someone else?' Jesus kept the men with him for some time so that they could see and hear his ministry in action, and then sent them back to tell John what they had seen and heard: 'the blind receive their sight, the lame walk, lepers are cleansed, and the deaf hear, the dead are raised up, the poor have good news preached to them' (Luke 7:22). He knew that John would recognise in this report an echo of the words in which the prophets of Israel had described the blessings of the age to come, and be reassured that he had not been mistaken when he hailed Jesus as the coming one.

In Jesus' message to John, the climax is reached in the declaration that 'the poor have good news preached to them'. John would probably recognise that this too was part of what the prophets had foretold when they spoke of the new age. In Isaiah 61:1 the prophet (or the person in whose name the prophet speaks) says, 'The Spirit of the Lord God is upon me, because the Lord has anointed me to bring good news to the poor' (or 'to the afflicted'). According to Luke, Jesus took these words as the text of the sermon which he preached in the synagogue at Nazareth at the beginning of his Galilaean ministry and applied them to the work on which he was embarking: 'Today', he said, 'this scripture has been fulfilled in your hearing' (Luke 4:21).

The 'bias to the poor' which these words reveal was nothing new in biblical religion. The poor were so greatly disadvantaged from the mere fact of their poverty that the God of Israel extended his special protection to them, in order to redress the unequal balance. Judges in Israel were directed to uphold the cause of the poor and those without natural protectors, like widows and orphans. This attitude was enshrined in the proverbial lore: 'He who is kind to the poor lends to the Lord, and he will repay him for his deed' (Proverbs 19:17) – words which provided the text for Dean Swift's famous one-sentence charity sermon: 'If you like the security, down with the dust!' So Jesus stood in the authentic prophetic tradition when he pronounced as the first of his beatitudes: 'Blessed are you who are poor; the kingdom of God is yours' (Luke 6:20).

The friend of sinners

It was not only to those who were financially poor that Jesus extended a special welcome. There were some who were reasonably well-off in material goods but deprived of respect, treated as outcasts from society, stigmatised as 'sinners' – sinners not in the general sense in which people will admit that 'we are all sinners' but in a sense which implied special disapproval. The sinners whom Jesus conspicuously befriended were regarded as anti-social, thoroughly disreputable types. Among these the tax-collectors of the day were regarded as particularly despicable. Whether they operated in the Roman province of Judaea or in Herod Antipas's Galilee, the system in which they were involved made it inevitable that they should exploit their neighbours, and many of them grew rich at their neighbours' expense. In popular esteem they were on a level with prostitutes. The term 'scab', as employed by a trade unionist in our society, expresses the same feeling of contempt and abhorrence as respectable people had for the tax-collectors and other 'sinners' with whom Jesus associated.

True, Jesus defended his practice by saying that it was sick people, not healthy people, who needed a doctor, and that similarly it was sinners, not righteous people, who needed his attention. But that argument did not satisfy his critics. He did not just tolerate the drop-outs to whom he ministered, holding his nose, so to speak, while he treated their moral wounds. He did not run a rescue mission for them or talk patronisingly to them. 'He went about doing good', as Peter said (Acts 10:38), but not in the manner of a professional 'do-gooder'. He accepted sinners, and they were glad to accept him. He was glad to share their meals, and they would certainly not have invited him to do so if they had suspected that the invitation might be disdainfully rejected or politely declined. He gave the impression, indeed, that he really enjoyed the company of such people – that he preferred it, in fact, to the company of those who had a good opinion of themselves. He probably felt more at home sitting at table with Levi the tax-collector than with Simon the Pharisee. Simon no doubt felt that he was honouring this itinerant prophet (if prophet he was) by inviting him to dinner, and he naturally took offence at the courtesy which his guest showed to a disreputable intruder who crept into the house after him and behaved in an embarrassingly unconventional way. There she sat at his feet, kissing them throughout the meal, without one word of remonstrance from him. Surely, thought Simon, if this man were a prophet, he would know this woman's character and forbid her to touch him. But she evidently recognised that Jesus understood her need and would help her without lecturing her or pursing his lips in disapproval of her present conduct or her general way of life. She and others like her knew him to be their friend, and showed their appreciation of him in ways that came naturally to them. Society condemned them, but he did not.[1]

All this was very disturbing to the moral majority of that day. That a prophet, a religious teacher, a holy man should act as he did was really letting the side down. It was difficult enough for them to maintain respectable standards in a wicked world, they felt, without this man's consorting with people for whom respectable standards did not exist. Their resentment found expression in frequently repeated remarks: 'He welcomes sinners; he actually sits at table with them!' (Luke 15:2). 'A glutton and a drunkard, a friend of tax collectors and sinners!' (Luke 7:34). A man, they implied, is known by the company he keeps.

But Jesus accepted such people as human beings who needed his healing touch as much as paralytics and lepers did. When he said to them, 'Your sins are forgiven; don't sin again', their subsequent life (we can well believe) was vastly different from what their life had been before, thanks to their encounter with him. The description 'the friend of sinners' is one of the most heart-warming designations given to him today; it takes an effort to realise that it was first given to him by way of disparagement, not appreciation.

Jesus claimed, moreover, that his attitude to outcasts and drop-outs was wholly in line with God's. This is emphasised in one after another of his parables. It was the tax-collector, whose lack of any sense of moral worth made him cast himself, sinner as he was, on the mercy of God, who went home 'justified'; not the man who lived a decent and disciplined life.[2] (Is it then futile to live a decent and disciplined life? No indeed, but it is dangerous to imagine that a decent and disciplined life establishes a claim on God's favour.) It was the black sheep of the family who was welcomed home with feasting, music and dancing, not the son who had never cost his father a moment's anxiety.[3] It was not a fellow-Jew who helped the half-dead man who had been mugged on the Jericho road, but one of those unspeakable Samaritans, a rank outsider, capable (it was believed) of any outrage against decent feeling.[4] (Why is 'Samaritan' a good word in our vocabulary? Because Jesus told the story of the good Samaritan. But those who first heard it must have felt as a Ballymena congregation might feel today, if the preacher told them how a member of the Ulster Defence Regiment had recently suffered serious injuries from an explosion on a road in South Armagh. A Church of Ireland clergyman and a Presbyterian elder both drove past, but judged it safer not to stop; it was a Sinn Feiner from the south who gave the man first aid and drove him to the nearest hospital.)

This association with sinners was bound up with Jesus' dedication of himself to do the will of God, of which he gave evidence in submitting to a baptism which was especially for sinners. It found its climax in his suffering and death, when he was 'numbered with transgressors' and laid down his life as a ransom for many.[5] Later in the first century, when fundamental tenets of Christian faith were summed up for readier circulation and repetition under the rubric 'This is a faithful saying', the first and most fundamental of these summaries ran thus: 'This is a faithful saying, worthy of universal acceptance: Christ Jesus came into the world to save *sinners*' (1 Timothy 1:15).

Chapter 5

Jesus and His Disciples

Jesus the teacher

As Jesus' ministry in Galilee proceeded, tension and conflict increased. His activity as a healer continued to make him very popular with the common people. He attached a number of young men to himself on a personal basis. These are known to us as his disciples. It was customary for the leading rabbis of the time to have a following of disciples, and other religious leaders had theirs. John the Baptist had a group of disciples whom he instructed in the 'way of righteousness' which he taught; we know that he gave them a form of prayer to repeat, but we do not know what it was.[1] They did what they could to serve him during his imprisonment by Antipas, and they perpetuated his teaching and his baptism after his death.

Jesus was popularly called 'rabbi' because he was recognised as a religious teacher, although he had never been a rabbinical disciple himself. His methods of teaching his disciples were different from those practised by most of the rabbis. In some rabbinical schools the method of learning was the word-for-word retention and repetition of what the master taught: one rabbi described the ideal student as 'a well-cemented cistern that never loses a drop'[2] (referring to cisterns dug in the rocky soil of Palestine to catch rainwater when it fell, the sides and floor being cemented or plastered to render them watertight). Some of Jesus' teaching was certainly given in an easily memorisable form, following the traditional patterns of Hebrew poetry; but his aim was that his disciples should grasp the basic principles of what he taught and use their discretion and initiative in communicating to others what they themselves had learned.

The tension and conflict which attended Jesus' ministry arose largely out of his disregard of the tradition of the elders, especially with regard to sabbath observance and the requirements of ritual purity. On sabbath observance he took the line that the sabbath was made for human beings and not vice versa, so that its observance should not stand in the way of men and women's health and general well-being. Anyone who shared meals so readily as he did with all sorts and conditions of people could obviously not take seriously the scrupulous rulings which laid down what food might and might not be eaten if the requirements of purity were not to be infringed. In Jesus' eyes, people rightly took precedence over regulations. In any case, it was not the things that went into the human stomach that conveyed real impurity, but the things that came out of the human heart – malicious, unclean and covetous thoughts, which resulted in evil behaviour.[3]

The teachers of the law and the synagogue authorities were quite unhappy about the line that Jesus took in these matters. More and more he found the synagogues closed to him as places where he might expound his teaching. But the mountain slope and the lakeside provided natural gathering-places for those who still came together in large numbers to hear him. There is one spot near Capernaum where the land rising from the water's edge forms a natural theatre, and if Jesus pushed out from shore a little way in a boat he could address the people from there without being jostled and be heard perfectly by those on the outermost fringes of the crowd.

The twelve apostles

After some months he selected from his disciples twelve men to carry his message throughout the Jewish areas of Galilee (and possibly further afield). These twelve men journeyed two by two; each pair would visit one town or village after another and proclaim the good news of the kingdom of God, healing the sick in Jesus' name. Their ministry was to be an extension of his.[4]

From the fact of their being 'sent' on this mission, these twelve men were called 'apostles' (special messengers). They had no authority of their own; their authority was derived from the one who commissioned them and could be exercised only within the terms of their commission. It was not on account of this particular commission that the apostles of Jesus who played such an influential part in the founding of the Christian church were so called. Most of the 'apostles' who were sent on this Galilaean mission, it is true, were also apostles at that later date, with more widespread and enduring terms of reference, but that was because he appeared to them in resurrection and recommissioned them.

The twelve apostles were mostly Galilaeans. One appears to have been a Judaean, if Judas's surname Iscariot means, as it most probably does, 'the man of Kerioth' (Kerioth being a place in the south of the old tribal territory of Judah, mentioned in Joshua 15:25). They seem to have been a bunch of rugged individualists. Peter's impetuous nature is well enough attested in the New Testament record. As for the two sons of Zebedee, James and John, it was not for nothing that Jesus called them *Boanê-rges*, 'the sons of thunder' or 'sons of tumult'. And what is to be made of the fact that another of the band was called Simon the Zealot? We should not conclude without more ado that he belonged – or had belonged – to the party of the Zealots, the anti-Roman party which maintained and put into practice the ideals of the 'fourth philosophy' first taught by that Judas the Galilaean who 'arose in the days of the census' (Acts 5:37).[5] It is not certain that this party was actually called the Zealot party much before AD 66, the year in which its members spear-headed the national revolt against Rome. The Greek word *zēlōtēs*, like the English word 'zealot', was in use as a common noun, with no special party sense; and this Simon may have possessed the temperament of a zealot to an even greater degree than many of his fellow-disciples. Luke is the only New Testament writer to designate him by the Greek word *zēlōtēs* (Luke 6:15; Acts 1:13). Mark, followed by Matthew, calls him the 'Cananaean' (Mark 3:18; Matthew 10:4). This word has nothing to do with 'Canaanite'; it is derived from the Aramaic *qan'ānā*, meaning 'zealot'. Luke does not care for foreign words; he likes to substitute Greek words with the same meaning (just as he substitutes the Greek word for 'skull' in Luke 23:33 for Golgotha, the corresponding Aramaic word, as the name of the place where Jesus was crucified). But why should Mark preserve the Aramaic form of Simon's sobriquet? Perhaps because, even at that early date, it had begun to bear something of its technical sense.

But even the inclusion of a Zealot (in the technical sense), or more probably a former Zealot, among the apostles should not be given too much significance. The inclusion of Simon the Zealot is balanced by the inclusion of Matthew the tax-collector, or rather the former tax-collector. A tax-collector was one of the most obnoxious representatives of the system which the Zealots were determined to smash. True, a tax-collector in Capernaum, where Matthew had his office, collected taxes not for the Roman Empire but for the administration of Herod Antipas – but Antipas was a creature of Rome. Yet Simon the Zealot and Matthew the tax-collector not only coexisted peacefully within the apostolic company but cooperated in the proclamation of the kingdom of God.

All three synoptic evangelists include Matthew in the list of the twelve, but the evangelist Matthew is the only one to call him 'Matthew the tax-collector'. He thus identifies him with the 'man called Matthew' whom, according to Matthew 9:9, Jesus found sitting at the tax office and called to follow him. Mark and Luke relate the same incident, but call the tax-collector Levi (Mark 2:14; Luke 5:27). There is nothing in their records to connect Levi the tax-collector with Matthew, whom they name as one of the twelve. There is a problem to be solved here, but this is not the place to offer a solution. The problem is compounded by Mark's calling the tax-collector 'the son of Alphaeus', for the lists of the twelve include a son of Alphaeus (whether the same Alphaeus or another man of the same name cannot be said) – James the less is distinguished from James the greater, the son of Zebedee, by being called 'James the son of Alphaeus'.

When Jesus sent the twelve out on their mission, he evidently expected that, wherever they went, they would find sympathisers willing to show them hospitality. To show hospitality to travelling preachers of righteousness was an acceptable act of charity. They had no need, therefore, to take provisions for the road. 'Whatever town or village you enter', said Jesus to them, 'find out who is worthy in it, and stay with him until you depart' (Matthew 10:11). This use of the adjective 'worthy' is interesting: it probably refers to people who were 'looking for the kingdom of God' and ready to entertain those who announced its approach. More generally, we may compare the situation of the twelve with that of the Essenes who, as Josephus tells us, had no need to take supplies with them when they went on a journey, since in every town they would find a member (or associate) of their order whose business it was to entertain travelling members of the brotherhood.[6]

Crisis in the wilderness

The twelve had a most encouraging reception on this mission, and when it was accomplished they were able to bring back a glowing report to Jesus. But in their enthusiasm they had evidently said unwise things which gave their hearers the wrong idea. They were understood to mean that the kingdom of God which they announced was about to displace existing regimes, including the rule of Herod Antipas in Galilee. Antipas had felt his authority threatened when John the Baptist denounced him, and slept more easily when John was safely out of the way. But now it looked as if he had a new John the Baptist on his hands. 'I beheaded John', he said, 'but who is this of whom I hear such things?' (Luke 9:9).

It would not be surprising if Antipas thought that his best

course would be to silence Jesus as he had silenced John. Realising this, Jesus took his disciples across the lake. There they were out of the jurisdiction of Antipas, in the tetrarchy of his brother Philip. Philip's subjects were mainly Gentiles, and not liable to be stirred to disaffection by expectations based on the oracles of Hebrew prophets.

But Jesus and the disciples were not allowed to enjoy quietness for long. Excited Galilaeans found out where they were, and came on them in their retreat east of the lake. They were leaderless men, eager for someone to put himself at their head and inaugurate the new order for which they were waiting. Jesus recognised this: in his eyes they were like sheep without a shepherd – which means not a congregation without a pastor but an army without a captain. He knew that if they found the wrong kind of captain they could be led to disaster. The kind of captain they wanted is shown in John's record: after Jesus had fed them there in the wilderness, they tried to force him to be their king (John 6:15). As their ancestors had been fed with manna in another wilderness under the leadership of the first Moses, so this man who had fed them here was the second Moses who would surely guide them to the promised land. But Jesus refused to be the kind of leader they wanted, and they had no use for the only kind of leader he was prepared to be. Many who had listened with avid attention to his message of the kingdom thus far now realised that he was not speaking of the kind of kingdom they desired, and in their disillusionment they no longer followed him in such numbers as before.

Jesus knew, moreover, that his own disciples were infected with the unhealthy excitement that had brought together this crowd of would-be freedom fighters.[7] He had to compel his disciples to sail back across the lake while he persuaded the crowd to disband. It was a critical moment in his ministry: he may well have recognised in it a recurrence of the wilderness temptation which had followed his baptism – the temptation to achieve his mission by the way of armed resistance rather than the way pointed out to him by his heavenly Father.

Peter's confession

Rejoining the twelve, Jesus took them on a circular journey away from Galilee, through Phoenician territory and back through the region belonging to the cities of the Decapolis (a federation of ten cities stretching from Damascus south to Philadelphia, the modern Amman). Now they had an opportunity of learning more about the character of the kingdom which they had recently been announcing, more about the goal towards which their master's ministry was directed. Towards the end of their journey, in the vicinity of Caesarea Philippi, near one of the sources of the Jordan, Jesus tested them to see how much they had learned.

Peter, acting (according to custom) as spokesman for the group, expressed the conviction that Jesus was the Messiah. In the circumstances, this was a more remarkable declaration than might be realised. There were various ideas in the air as to the kind of person the Messiah would be and the kind of things he would do, but it is not clear that Jesus conformed to any of those ideas. He certainly did not conform to one popular idea, which was that the Messiah would lead his people in a campaign of liberation against the occupying power of Rome and establish a new order for Israel which would match, and even surpass, the achievement of David and Solomon a thousand years before. An expectation of this kind seems to have been in the minds of some at least of the disciples. Those who thought this way must have wondered why their master had turned down a golden opportunity of putting himself at the head of an army of willing patriots and leading them to victory over their oppressors.

If now Peter and his companions confessed Jesus to be the Messiah, this meant that the idea of the Messiah was coming to be filled in their minds with the character and policy of Jesus as they knew him. Here we have, in fact, the beginning of the process by which the term 'Messiah', and even more its equivalent 'Christ', acquired in Christian thinking and language the meaning of the name of Jesus. If 'Messiah' is the designation given to God's agent for the fulfilment of his purpose in the world, then the confession that Jesus is the Messiah means that Jesus is just that – God's agent for the fulfilment of his purpose in the world,

the Proper Man,
Whom God himself hath bidden.

If Peter and the others were beginning to grasp this, then they must learn more. What is the nature of God's purpose in the world, and what is the manner of its fulfilment?

'The Son of Man must suffer'

According to the Gospel of Mark, it was now that Jesus began to tell his disciples that 'the Son of Man must suffer many things, and be rejected' (Mark 8:31), that suffering and rejection were indeed the means by which he was to fulfil his messianic mission. They would not have been ready for this disconcerting revelation before Peter's confession; in fact, they were not really ready for it then, and it had to be repeated and emphasised. The Son of Man would be manifested in glory, 'But first he must suffer many things and be rejected by this generation' (Luke 17:25). The necessity of this was underlined by the fact that it was the subject of prophetic scripture: 'how is it *written* of the Son of Man, that he should suffer many things and be treated with contempt?' (Mark 9:12).

So unprepared for such news as this were the disciples that, when Jesus first began to speak in this way, Peter took him by the arm and begged him not to say such things: 'Bless you, Master!' he said, 'This is never going to happen to you.' But Jesus told him sharply that he was looking at the situation from a merely human viewpoint, and not seeing it from God's side; he went so far as to repel Peter's well-meant expostulation with a retort similar to the language he had used in repelling the wilderness temptations: 'Get behind me, Satan!' (Mark 8:33). He recognised that Peter, for all his good intentions, was trying to turn him aside from what he knew to be God's will for him.

If the disciples had begun to follow him in the expectation that he would lead them to victory and power as the words were commonly understood, it was necessary that they should have the situation put before them plainly, so that they would have no ground for complaining that he had enlisted them under false pretences. If from Caesarea Philippi onwards he told them of his impending rejection and death, it was similarly from then on that he warned them that anyone who persisted in following him must 'take up his cross' in order to do so. To take up one's cross was not in those days a figure of speech for inconvenience or harassment; the picture which the words conjured up was too horribly familiar. A man who took up his cross did so in order to carry it to the place of execution and be fastened to it there. But if that was the kind of experience which Jesus envisaged for himself, those who followed him could reasonably expect to share it. To turn back now would be to save their lives in the short term, but it would mean the losing of their lives in the light of the final assessment, which would lie with the Son of Man himself.

Nearly two thousand years later, as we look back on their decision, we can make a provisional and limited assessment of our own. Their decision was the right one. If they had turned back then, nothing more would have been heard of them. They counted the cost and continued to follow Jesus, and their memory is honoured to this day. We may pronounce the verdict of history; the verdict of eternity lies in other hands.

Chapter
6

The Son of Man

The representative Man

When Jesus, as reported by Mark, told his disciples that the Son of Man must suffer, and went on to indicate that this was something which had been 'written' concerning him, his disciples appear to have understood at once that he was speaking about himself. This may have been because they were accustomed to hearing him refer to himself as 'the Son of Man'. We do not know if this self-designation conveyed any particular significance to them. Modern readers of the Gospels are familiar with the expression on Jesus' lips, and rarely pause to ask why he should have referred to himself in this strangely allusive way. On the other hand, there is no subject on which specialist students of the Gospels have written at greater length, but there is no unanimity among them on the origin or meaning of the expression.

Unlike the disciples, the crowds who gathered to hear Jesus teaching in the temple precincts in Jerusalem in the week preceding his arrest and execution were not accustomed to the use of the self-designation 'the Son of Man' by Jesus or by anyone else. When therefore they heard him say that 'the Son of Man must be lifted up' (the equivalent in John's language to Mark's 'the Son of Man must suffer'), they asked 'Who is this Son of Man?' (John 12:34). It was a better question than they realised, for the answer to it leads to the heart of the mystery of Jesus' identity.

With one significant exception, the phrase 'the Son of Man'

is found in the New Testament only on Jesus' lips. (The Jerusalem crowd's question, 'Who is this Son of Man?' is not really an exception, because it was simply an echo of Jesus' own words.) The significant exception is its use by Stephen, an early Jerusalem Christian, towards the end of his trial before the high priest and his colleagues: 'I see the heavens opened', he said, 'and the Son of Man standing at the right hand of God' (Acts 7:56). The significance of this exception will appear later.[1]

As used by Jesus, the expression 'the Son of Man' is sometimes a general self-designation; at other times it bears a special relation to his earthly ministry or to his coming glory. It was not a form of words which already had associations for his hearers. Many of them would immediately have understood, or would have thought they understood, a reference to the Messiah: they would have supposed that the great king of the future, the descendant of David, was meant. For this very reason, perhaps, Jesus did not go around claiming to be the Messiah; even when Peter made his confession at Caesarea Philippi the disciples were strictly forbidden to tell anyone that Jesus was the Messiah. But 'the Son of Man' was not a title in general currency; Jesus could use it without fear of being misunderstood.

When he used it as a general self-designation, it was practically equivalent to the pronoun 'I'. On one occasion he contrasted himself with the ascetic John the Baptist, who came 'eating no bread and drinking no wine', and said 'The Son of Man has come eating and drinking' (Luke 7:34). It is difficult to see any difference in meaning between that last statement and '*I* have come eating and drinking.' The evangelists themselves sometimes appear to treat 'the Son of Man' and 'I' on Jesus' lips as interchangeable. For example, Mark says that Jesus asked his disciples at Caesarea Philippi, 'Who do the people say I am?' whereas Matthew phrases his question: 'Who do the people say the Son of Man is?' (Mark 8:27; Matthew 16:13).

Jesus normally spoke in Aramaic, and in that language the expression meaning 'a man' is literally 'a son of man'. So, in

the ears of Aramaic speakers 'the Son of Man' might be taken
to mean simply 'the man'. If the evangelists, who reported
Jesus' words in Greek, preserved the un-Greek phrase 'the
Son of Man' instead of translating it as 'the man', it was
probably because they recognised that there was something
distinctive in his use of it.

It is unlikely that Jesus simply used the expression as some
speakers today use the indefinite pronoun 'one', in order to
avoid the personal 'I'. It has been held that in Aramaic the
expression could have the more definite force of 'this man'
(meaning 'I myself'), and sometimes indeed this may be its
force when used by Jesus (as when he said that 'the Son of
Man has come eating and drinking').

At other times, it has been suggested, the expression means
'man' in general – man as opposed to God on the one hand or
to the beasts on the other hand. Why, for example, did Jesus
say that it is more pardonable to speak against the Son of Man
than to speak against the Holy Spirit? Possibly in the original
form of the saying a contrast was made between the venial sin
of speaking against 'man' or human beings in general and the
'eternal sin' of speaking against the Spirit of God (Mark
3:28,29).[2] Some have thought they detected an instance of
this kind in the place where the Son of Man, in contrast to the
foxes and the birds, is said to have 'nowhere to lay his head'
(Matthew 8:20; Luke 9:58). But this is improbable: it is not
true that human beings are distinguished from the wild animals in having no home of their own. Here, certainly, Jesus
was applying the term 'the Son of Man' to himself in relation
to his earthly ministry, during which he had no fixed abode
and was as likely to spend the night on a hillside under the
stars as in a bed under a roof.[3]

In Mark's record most of the 'Son of Man' sayings of Jesus
come after the Caesarea Philippi incident. But there are two
important ones which come earlier. The first of these occurs in
the story of Jesus' healing the paralysed man who was let
down through the roof of a house in Capernaum. Before
healing his paralysis, Jesus assured him that his sins were
forgiven, and when some of those present were scandalised at

his doing so, he declared that 'the Son of Man has authority on earth to forgive sins' (Mark 2:10). Plainly he was exercising this authority in his own person, but when he claimed to exercise it as the Son of Man, the phrase may mean something like the representative man. Matthew evidently understood his words in this sense, for in his account of the incident he says that the crowds 'glorified God, who had given such authority to human beings' (Matthew 9:8) – 'human beings' or 'men' being an instance of what grammarians call the generalising plural. The idea behind this use of the phrase 'Son of Man' is similar to what Paul had in mind when he spoke of Jesus as 'the last Adam' or 'the second man' (1 Corinthians 15:45,47). The first Adam bore a name which means 'mankind' because he was the representative man; this role has been taken over and raised to a new dimension by Jesus. The forgiveness of sins is a prerogative of God, and he has been pleased to share it with the Son of Man.[4]

The phrase appears again, and to much the same effect, in the report of an early sabbath controversy. When fault was found with Jesus' disciples because they plucked ears of grain as they walked through the fields on a sabbath day and rubbed them in their hands to extract the kernel, the point of the complaint was that they were technically performing two kinds of work that were forbidden on the sabbath – plucking being a form of reaping and rubbing being a form of grinding. But Jesus replied that the sabbath was not ordained for the inconvenience of human beings but for their convenience: 'The sabbath was made for man, not man for the sabbath; so the Son of Man is lord even of the sabbath' (Mark 2:27,28). If the sabbath was made for man, then it is as the representative man that Jesus disposes of the sacred day with such sovereign authority. He acts and speaks as the one whom God has appointed to be spokesman and sponsor of the race for whose benefit the sabbath rest was instituted.[5]

'The Son of Man came . . .'

Some of the 'Son of Man' sayings express Jesus' purpose in life: 'the Son of Man came' to do this or that. 'The Son of Man came to seek and to save the lost' (Luke 19:10). 'The Son of Man came not to be served but to serve, and to give his life as a ransom for many' (Mark 10:45).

This latter saying is of special importance. It reminds many readers of the Servant of the Lord in the book of Isaiah, who is said to have given his life as a sin-offering and to have borne 'the sin of many' (Isaiah 53:10–12). It does not reproduce the actual wording of the description of the Servant, but it certainly echoes the sense.

With this saying we must associate those sayings which insist that 'the Son of Man must suffer', and especially that saying which speaks of the suffering and rejection of the Son of Man as something that is 'written' concerning him (Mark 9:12). Why *must* the Son of Man suffer? Because he was set on a collision course with the authorities? Possibly; but why should he consider this collision course, with its violent end, to be inevitable? Because this was spelt out plainly in those scriptures where he found his own programme mapped out. It was 'written' that the Son of Man should 'suffer many things and be treated with contempt'; but where was it so written? There are passages here and there in the Old Testament, especially in the Psalms, which depict a righteous person enduring unjust suffering, and enduring it for God's sake; and there is evidence that some of those passages played a part in Jesus' thinking about his own experience. But the themes of service, suffering and giving one's life as a ransom or sin-offering come together in Isaiah 52:13–53:12 in such a way as to suggest that it is here pre-eminently that it is 'written' that the Son of Man should suffer.

Why should Jesus see his life-mission laid out before him in this particular prophecy? There are two passages in the book of Isaiah which are introduced with the words (spoken by God): 'Behold my servant'. This passage (Isaiah 52:13–53:12) is one of them: it portrays the Servant of the Lord as misrepresented, afflicted, 'despised and rejected by men', ill-treated and put to death, but presenting his life to God as an atonement for the guilt of others, bringing them renewal through his suffering, and ultimately being vindicated and highly exalted. The other is the first passage where the Servant appears (Isaiah 42:1–4); it opens with the words: 'Behold my servant, whom I uphold, my chosen, in whom my soul delights; I have put my Spirit upon him'. When Jesus received the Spirit of God as he emerged from the baptismal water of the Jordan, these were the words which he recognised as the heavenly voice addressed him, and here, he knew, his life-mission was expressed. The two passages opening with the words 'Behold my servant' were closely related in his mind; the former was to be interpreted in the fuller language of the latter.

It was not merely a matter of conforming his life henceforth to a written programme. To serve his Father, whose will had been so clearly revealed to him, and to bring the utmost aid and blessing to men and women – this was in any case the dearest desire of his heart. But the fact that this kind of ministry was clearly depicted in the prophetic writings as the way of serving God confirmed the necessity of its being fulfilled, with the rejection and suffering that it would involve. Jesus' personal conviction that the scriptures had to be fulfilled, and fulfilled in him, is embedded in the gospel records.

Through rejection to glory

In his proclamation of the kingdom of God, Jesus distinguished two phases. There was the present phase, manifested in his own works of mercy and power, but operating even so under limitations; and there was a future phase, soon to be realised, when it would 'come with power' (Mark 9:1). Similarly he distinguished the present condition of the Son of Man, disregarded and humiliated, from his future investment with glory, more or less as the prophet had contrasted the insult and injury meted out to the Servant of the Lord with his coming vindication, when he would be 'exalted and extolled and made very high' (Isaiah 52:13).

The Son of Man, according to the words of Jesus, will in days to come enjoy a position of unique authority in the Father's presence. Not only so, but those who have shared the Son of Man's humiliation will then be acknowledged by him; those who have disregarded him now will receive no recognition from him then. 'Whoever is ashamed of me and of my words in this adulterous and sinful generation, of him will the Son of Man also be ashamed, when he comes in the glory of his Father with the holy angels' (Mark 8:38). But 'every one who acknowledges me before men', he said, 'the Son of Man also will acknowledge before the angels of God' (Luke 12:8).

It is in the light of these last words that we can best understand the one New Testament text where someone other than Jesus spontaneously employs the phrase 'the Son of Man'. When Stephen saw 'the Son of Man standing at the right hand of God', he saw him standing there as his advocate. Stephen, condemned by an earthly court, appealed to the judgment of the heavenly court. He had acknowledged Jesus as Lord before men, and now (as promised) the Son of Man rose up as his advocate to acknowledge him before God. (In Luke 12:8 the phrase 'before the angels of God' is another way of saying 'before God'.)

The sayings about the Son of Man's investment with glory help us to discern the most probable Old Testament background of the designation as Jesus used it. The Son of Man who is to come 'in the glory of his Father with the holy angels' is that 'one like a son of man' whom Daniel, in a vision of the day of judgment, saw coming 'with the clouds of heaven' into the presence of God, the 'Ancient of Days', and receiving universal and eternal sovereignty from him (Daniel 7:13,14). The definite article in '*the* Son of Man' (in Jesus' usage) is emphatic: the reference is to that particular human figure seen by Daniel. In Daniel's Aramaic 'one like a son of man' means a being of human appearance. It is implied, if not expressly stated, that in Daniel's vision this being was en-

throned alongside the Ancient of Days. There was no difficulty, then, in linking Daniel's vision with the oracle of
Psalm 110:1, where someone whom the psalmist calls 'my
lord' is invited by God to sit at his right hand. Jesus, as we
shall see, linked these two scriptures when the high priest of
Israel challenged him to declare his identity.[6]

There is one place in the Gospels where the definite article
is missing from the designation on Jesus' lips. In John 5:27 the
Father is said to have given the Son 'authority to execute
judgment, because he is Son of Man'. The absence of the
definite article before 'Son of Man' in this place has no
theological significance; it is a matter of Greek grammatical
usage.

The background of this saying is evidently Daniel's vision
just referred to, where the sovereignty divinely conferred on
the 'one like a son of man' includes the authority to execute
judgment. Nor is there any doubt about the person who is said
in John 5:27 to be 'Son of Man'; it is to 'the Son' that 'the
Father' has given this judicial authority. When 'the Son' and
'the Father' are spoken of together like this in the Gospels,
'the Son' is the Son of the Father, the Son of God. John, to a
greater degree than the other evangelists, presents the ministry of the earthly Jesus in the light of what he has come to
know about the heavenly Christ. But could one infer from
other biblical writers that 'the Son of Man' is in fact 'the Son of
God'?

Indeed one could. For one thing, if the scene depicted in
Daniel 7:13,14, is viewed in the light of ancient Near Eastern
imagery, one can only with difficulty escape the conclusion
that the 'one like a son of man' is greeted by the Ancient of
Days as his firstborn son. There are parallels here and there
in the Psalms – not only in Psalm 110:1, which has been
mentioned, but in other places where God acclaims and
installs the 'man of his right hand' as his son, his firstborn, 'the
highest of the kings of the earth' (Psalms 2:7; 80:17; 89:20
–27). In the synoptic Gospels, even when 'the Son of Man' is
Jesus' self-designation in humiliation, the note of authority
attaching to it is not difficult to detect. It becomes clearest of

all in his response to the high priest's question about his identity, as his judges perceived very well. Luke, in his report of Jesus' trial, brings this out by saying that when Jesus declared that from now on the Son of Man would be 'seated at the right hand of the power of God' they all replied, 'Are you the Son of God, then?' (Luke 22:69,70). He did not need to claim in so many words that he was the Son of God; that was implied in what he had just said about the Son of Man.

It might be suggested, in fact, that the question 'Who is this Son of Man?' received its answer when the Roman centurion at the crucifixion of Jesus, impressed by the manner of his death, said 'Truly this man was the Son of God!' (Mark 15:39). But to this we must return.[7]

For the present let it be said that 'the Son of Man' was Jesus' way of referring to himself and his mission – a form of words that had no antecedent significance for his hearers, so that he could fill it with whatever meaning he chose – representative man, righteous sufferer, obedient servant of God, or the one foreordained to be invested with universal authority.

Chapter
7

Jesus' Way of Life

The sermon on the mount

What way of life did Jesus recommend to his followers? It was a way that rose directly from his proclamation of the kingdom of God, a way that he recommended not only by word but by example. The kingdom of God, the divine rule, could not be effectively established on earth until after the death and vindication of Jesus himself, but even while it was in process of inauguration through his ministry its principles could be accepted and put into action in the lives of his followers, who thus became 'children of the kingdom'.[1] The ethical principles of the kingdom of God, as Jesus gave them utterance, are found especially in the collection of his sayings called the 'sermon on the mount' (Matthew 5–7). These sayings were addressed to his disciples; their aim was not to show how human beings in general ought to live so as to bring in the kingdom of God, but rather what were the attitudes and practices that should be seen in those who were already children of the kingdom.

It is true, but pointless, to say that the world would be a happier place if everybody practised the teaching of the sermon on the mount. It would be a happier place, indeed, if everybody obeyed the ten commandments; but those who find the standard of the ten commandments difficult to attain are not likely to have much success in coping with the higher standard of the sermon on the mount. The sermon on the mount takes up where the ten commandments leave off. 'You shall not kill', says one of the ten commandments, but the sermon on the mount says that anyone who is angry with his brother (or her sister) stands in danger of divine judgment (because the murderous act would not take place if it were not preceded by the angry thought). 'You shall not commit adultery', says another of the ten commandments, but the sermon on the mount finds the root of the trouble in the adulterous thought and desire from which the overt act of adultery springs.[2]

In Jesus' ministry the kingdom of God was already at work, but it had not yet come 'with power' (Mark 9:1). There is thus a certain 'interim' quality about Jesus' ministry before his death and resurrection, and some have insisted that this interim quality attaches to his ethical teaching – that he taught, in short, an 'interim ethic' which was not intended to have permanent validity.

One scholar who maintained this view was the great Albert Schweitzer.[3] But there was a delightful paradox about Schweitzer's position on this subject. Schweitzer the theologian believed that the coming of the kingdom, in the form in which Jesus expected it, was a noble delusion. Logically, then, one could not take seriously the interim ethic which Jesus laid down for his followers to practise in the brief interval before the consummation which never arrived. But it was precisely this interim ethic which provided the motive power for Schweitzer the missionary when he abandoned the prospects of professional advancement in theology, medicine or music to spend the greater part of his life in the service of God and his fellow-men in West Africa. For the ministry of Jesus *is* the kingdom of God; it is not a mere prelude to it. The kingdom of God was inaugurated in power by the death and resurrection of Jesus because the ministry of Jesus was crowned in his death and resurrection and has continued in the world ever since. His disciples did not succeed to the ministry which he bequeathed to them: it is still *his* ministry, but he shares it with them through his Spirit. And because it is still his ministry, the ethical principles which marked it in its first phase still mark it in its present phase.

It is necessary, of course, to consider the ethical teaching of Jesus in relation to its contemporary context; only so shall we be able to relate it properly to other contexts. Its primary context includes the social, political and religious state of Palestine under the Roman Empire in the earlier first century AD. Much of its detail is intelligible only in this setting. For example, it is much more concerned with the situation of subjects than with the situation of rulers. Only rarely did Jesus have the opportunity of speaking to rulers. But that does not really impair the relevance of his teaching; to this day, there are many more subjects than rulers in the world. Again, the people among whom Jesus lived were not members of a democracy, who had some say in electing their rulers and therefore some responsibility for what their elected rulers did; the rulers under whom they lived exercised their authority quite arbitrarily. Does it follow, then, that people today who live under despotic governments find that the teaching of Jesus speaks in some respects more directly to their condition than it does to those who are entitled periodically to throw out a government which has failed to give satisfaction? Perhaps it does.

The two great commandments

Jesus emphasised the ethical character of the Old Testament law by summarising it in terms of two of its commandments: 'You shall love the Lord your God with all your heart . . .' (Deuteronomy 6:5) and 'You shall love your neighbour as yourself' (Leviticus 19:18). The second of these was otherwise formulated in the Golden Rule: 'whatever you wish that men would do to you, do so to them; for this is the law and the prophets' (Matthew 7:12). Those last words are similar to the words by which Jesus commented on the twin commandments of love to God and love to human beings: 'On these two commandments depend all the law and the prophets' (Matthew 22:40).[4]

It is plain, then, that Jesus did not claim to be promulgating a new ethical code; he was restating the ethical requirements already laid down in the Old Testament. And indeed, he was not the only one to single out these two commandments as comprising the essence of the law of Moses; the Gospels themselves bear witness to this. The parable of the good Samaritan, says Luke, was told to an exponent of that law who asked Jesus how he might inherit eternal life. When Jesus asked him what the law said, he replied by quoting these two commandments. 'You are right', said Jesus, 'do that and you will find life.' But the man was not altogether satisfied. If God was to be loved, he knew who God was; if his neighbour was to be loved, then, he asked, 'Who is my neighbour?' (Luke 10:29). It was in answer to that question that Jesus told the story of the good Samaritan: my neighbour is the person who needs my help.

The occasion on which Jesus himself is reported to have summarised the whole law in the two great commandments of love was when a scribe, a student of the scriptures, came to him while he was teaching in the temple court during his last visit to Jerusalem and asked 'Which commandment is the first of all?' A variety of answers might have been given to that question: Jesus cited the commandment enjoining perfect love to God and added that there was another that stood beside it – the commandment of love to one's neighbour. The scribe agreed enthusiastically, and added that to love God with all the heart, and to love one's neighbour as oneself, was 'much more than all whole burnt offerings and sacrifices' (Mark 12:33). To say this in close proximity to the altar where burnt offerings and sacrifices were presented to God in accordance with the law of Israel showed sound insight into the things that mattered most; no wonder that Jesus welcomed his response and assured him that he was not far from the kingdom of God.

Jesus radicalised the requirements of the Old Testament law by applying them to the inner motive as well as to the outward word or action. He imparted a distinctiveness and freshness to his exposition of them as he made pronouncements on his personal authority – 'You have heard that it was

said . . . but *I* say to you . . .' – and affirmed that only in
paying heed to his words and putting them into practice could
men and women lay a secure foundation for life.

Jesus and the law of Moses

When it came to interpreting and applying specific commandments, Jesus did not follow the procedure of contemporary
rabbis. Indeed, he dismissed their rulings, handed down to
one generation from another by word of mouth, as too often
prone to obscure or frustrate the original intention for which
the commandments were given. He appealed back to that
original intention against the 'tradition of the elders';[5] he held
that a commandment was most worthily kept when its original
purpose was fulfilled.

If it was a question of observing the fourth commandment,
which safeguarded the sanctity of the sabbath day, what was
the original purpose for which the sabbath was ordained? It
was ordained for the rest, refreshment and relief of human
beings (and of animals too, for that matter); therefore, any
action which promoted those ends was a fitting action to be
performed on the sabbath. It was by this consideration that
Jesus defended his frequent performance of acts of healing on
this day. Those who criticised him in this matter would have
agreed that, in a life-or-death situation, suitable medical aid
should be given even on the sabbath; but those who could
easily wait another day or two should wait until the sabbath
was over. 'There are six days on which work ought to be
done', said one ruler of the synagogue, 'come on those days
and be healed, and not on the sabbath day' (Luke 13:14). But
Jesus disagreed: whether there was urgency or not, the
sabbath was a specially appropriate day on which to heal
people, because that was so completely in keeping with the
Creator's purpose in instituting the sabbath. An act of healing
did not desecrate the sabbath but honoured it, and honoured
the Creator himself at the same time.

We can recognise the working of the same principle in

Jesus' response to the question of divorce. It is assumed in the law of Deuteronomy that a husband is permitted to divorce his wife if he finds 'some indecency' or 'some unseemliness' in her (Deuteronomy 24:1). The rabbinical schools disagreed on the nature of this 'indecency' or 'unseemliness'; some interpreted it narrowly, others quite broadly. When Jesus was asked for a ruling on the subject, he ruled out divorce altogether. But why? Did Moses not authorise it? Yes, but that was a concession on Moses' part to the hardness of men's hearts; it formed no part of the Creator's purpose in instituting marriage. When he instituted marriage, it was in order that husband and wife might become so closely joined together as to constitute 'one flesh' (Genesis 2:24). 'What therefore God has joined together', said Jesus, 'let not man put asunder' (Mark 10:9).

In ruling thus, Jesus was not being a 'rigorist' and he certainly had no thought of laying down canon law. He was concerned to insist on the divine intention underlying the institution of marriage. His ruling, moreover, safeguarded the interests of women. In Jewish law the initiative in divorce lay with the husband; the balance was tilted one-sidedly against the wife, and Jesus' ruling had the effect of redressing this unequal balance.

It is plain enough that in the sermon on the mount Jesus was not imposing a set of statutes which could be enforced by material sanctions; he was prescribing a way of life for his followers. 'It would be a great point gained', said James Denney, 'if people would only consider that it was a Sermon, and was *preached*, not an *act* which was passed.'[6] Even so, Jesus made it clear to his disciples that more was expected of them than the ordinary morality of decent people, more even than the righteousness 'of the scribes and Pharisees' (Matthew 5:20). 'If you love those who love you, what credit is that to you? For even sinners love those who love them' (Luke 6:32). The message of the kingdom of God calls for acts of love to enemies and words of blessing and good will to ill-wishers and persecutors. The children of the kingdom should not insist on their rights but cheerfully relinquish them in the interests of the supreme law of love.

Non-violence

The way of non-violence is inculcated in all the strands of Jesus' teaching, including the earliest. Those who nevertheless maintain that Jesus advocated armed rebellion against the Romans, or at least sympathised with those who engaged in it, have a hard task in the light of the evidence. To turn the other cheek when one is wantonly punched on the jaw is not a natural reaction, but everyone knows that this is what Jesus inculcated. How does everyone know that? Not simply because there is a text in the Gospels (found both in Matthew 5:39 and in Luke 6:29) where these words are ascribed to him, but even more because these words express his general teaching and example where the proper response to malice and hostility is in view. If he did in fact recommend armed rebellion, then this aspect of his teaching must have been painstakingly weeded out of the gospel tradition at a very early date – within twenty years at most – and replaced by a pervasive picture of one who taught and practised non-resistance to evil. It is not for those who live in a free society to condemn others who feel that their only course of action against an oppressive regime is to take up arms against it; but such people are mistaken if they think they can claim the authority of Jesus for their armed resistance.

Jesus refers to men of violence who tried to seize the kingdom of God and bring it in by force, but he gives no hint that he approves of their policy or methods. On the contrary, he recommended the harder way of peace and submission. His followers were not to retaliate against injustice or oppression but rather to repay evil with good, to go a second mile when their services were commandeered for one mile. If this way of peace was repudiated in favour of the way of resistance and rebellion, disaster would follow. On one occasion Jesus was told of Galilaean pilgrims to Jerusalem who were involved in some disturbance and were cut down by Roman soldiers in the temple precincts. (A Roman garrison was quartered in the Antonia fortress, north-west of the temple area, from which two flights of steps led down into the outer court of the temple; if anything like a riot broke out, it could be put down by immediate military intervention.) Jesus' informants perhaps expected from him some expression of indignant sympathy with fellow-Galilaeans massacred while they were engaged in their sacrificial worship. What he actually said, however, was: 'Unless you undergo a change of heart, you will all be destroyed in the same way' (Luke 13:3). This may imply that the unfortunate Galilaeans had been caught up in a demonstration against the Roman government, and thereby constitute a warning to others that the same spirit of resistance in them will bring them to comparable destruction.

The imperial power of Rome was not experienced so directly in Galilee as in Judaea, and it was when he visited Judaea and, in particular, Jerusalem that Jesus spoke out most urgently on this issue. He wept over Jerusalem because it could not recognise the path of peace; the spirit of insurgency, with which so many of its residents sympathised, could only lead them all to unimaginable disaster.

The division which Jesus foresaw in society, and even within families, when some members followed him and some did not, inhered in the nature of the situation. That was the sense in which he said he had 'not come to bring peace, but a sword' (Matthew 10:34). He did not regard such division as desirable in itself. What was desirable was that those members of society, or members of families, who had embraced his way should not themselves be affected by the spirit of division but let their light so shine that the others would be attracted to it. This was one way in which the leaven of the kingdom of God should work until it had spread through the whole of society. But until it did so, tension and division would be the order of the day. Jesus' own experience provides a paradigm of this. While he was still an infant, Simeon of Jerusalem foretold that he would be 'a sign that is spoken against' (Luke

2:34); and the cross bears witness to the truth of Simeon's
prophecy.

Incentives

Various incentives are held out by Jesus as he recommends
the way of the kingdom of God as the path to be followed.
They include the prospect of reward or retribution at the last
judgment or in the course of history. Any courting of human
applause is discouraged: actions which are in themselves good
are deprived of any virtue if they are done 'before men in
order to be seen by them' (Matthew 6:1). But the highest of all
incentives is the example of God himself: his children should
reflect their Father's character. This incentive is clearly set
forth in the Old Testament: one section of the book of
Leviticus is commonly called 'the law of holiness' because of
its recurring refrain: 'I am the Lord your God . . . you shall
therefore be holy, for I am holy' (Leviticus 11:44,45). 'You,
therefore, must be perfect', says Jesus in the sermon on the
mount, 'as your heavenly Father is perfect' (Matthew 5:48).
In this context 'perfect' means something like 'all-embracing
in your love'. This injunction has a parallel in Luke 6:36, 'Be
merciful, even as your Father is merciful.' Something very
similar to this is found in an Aramaic paraphrase of Leviticus
22:28, where humane treatment of animals is enjoined: 'As
our Father is merciful in heaven, so you must be merciful on
earth.'[7] There was nothing, then, in this part of the sermon
which Jesus' Jewish hearers would find unfamiliar. They
would readily appreciate his argument that, if God does
not discriminate between the good and the bad in sending his
gifts of sunshine and rain, his children should equally show
kindness to all. It is, of course, one thing to appreciate
the argument; it is another thing, whether for Jews or for
Christians, to act accordingly.

The Gospels bear witness to the fact that Jesus' own life was
the practical manifestation of his teaching. This testimony
is specially explicit with regard to service and sacrifice.

Repeatedly he insisted that the highest honour lies in humble service – not as a reward for it, but in the service itself. In the kingdoms of the world the high and mighty received service; this was a sign of the honour in which they were held. Jesus' disciples found it difficult to grasp the thought that it is quite otherwise in the kingdom of God. 'It shall not be so among you', he said to them, 'but whoever would be great among you must be your servant, and whoever would be first among you must be slave of all. For the Son of Man also came not to be served but to serve, and to give his life as a ransom for many' (Mark 10:43–45).[8]

Luke reports him as saying to his disciples at the last supper, 'I am among you as one who serves' (Luke 22:27); and John tells how on the same occasion he suited the action to the word and washed their feet at the beginning of the meal. This was a service which any one of them would gladly have performed for him; but none of them would willingly have done it for his fellow-disciples, because it would have been regarded as an admission of inferiority. Jesus' action set the whole principle of service in a new light, and presented them with an example to follow: 'If I then, your Lord and Teacher, have washed your feet, you also ought to wash one another's feet' (John 13:14).

Chapter
8

Jesus in Jerusalem

Visits to Jerusalem

Throughout the main phase of his Galilaean ministry Jesus appears not to have visited Jerusalem. The Gospel of John represents him as being a frequent visitor to Jerusalem, but makes it plain that the feeding of the multitude east of the lake of Galilee took place at the Passover season, and Jesus was certainly not in Jerusalem on that occasion.

There were three outstanding festivals in the Jewish year when large numbers of people, not only from Palestine but also from the lands of the dispersion, made a religious pilgrimage to Jerusalem to take part in the special services held in the temple on those occasions. These were the week-long Festival of Unleavened Bread, introduced by the Passover meal, which coincided with a full moon in March or April; the Festival of Pentecost, which fell seven weeks later; and the Festival of Tabernacles or Booths, lasting eight days, which began six months after Passover, in the autumn of the year. These festivals were originally associated with the agricultural year, but had come in addition to commemorate events in the early history of Israel.

When Jesus left Galilee for the last time with the twelve and some other disciples, they set out for Judaea and arrived in Jerusalem during the Festival of Tabernacles in the autumn of (probably) AD 29. For the next six months they remained in Judaea or Peraea (across the Jordan), visiting Jerusalem occasionally, as for the Festival of Dedication in December.[1]

On his visits to Jerusalem Jesus taught those who gathered round him in the outer court of the temple. Several rabbis had 'teaching pitches' there, and Jesus' presence led to debates between him and them, and also between him and the temple authorities.

The temple authorities were closely related to the chief-priestly establishment, which depended for its survival on the good will of the Roman administration of Judaea. They were naturally nervous at the activity of an unconventional teacher who seemed to be gathering a large and enthusiastic body of followers; the enthusiasm engendered by his teaching was apt to get out of hand and invite suppression by the Roman forces. The Roman forces pulled no punches when it came to suppressing popular demonstrations; innocent bystanders were likely to be hurt as well as those primarily responsible for the demonstrations. Mention has been made already of some Galilaean pilgrims who were cut down in the temple precincts not long before, when they were taking part in one of the sacred festivals and had got caught up in some disturbance.[2] Jesus might preach a gospel of peace, but any talk of a new kingdom could excite revolutionary sentiments among the people.

But as Jesus had proclaimed his message in Galilee, so Judaea also – and pre-eminently Jerusalem, 'the city of the great King' – must have the opportunity of hearing the true way of peace. The position of the chief-priestly establishment and the temple authorities might be dependent on their retaining diplomatic relations with the Roman governor and his staff, but that meant that the Jewish establishment became almost as unpopular as the Roman government. Jesus was concerned to emphasise to the people of Jerusalem that, if their minds remained bent on resistance to Rome, disaster would overtake their city and themselves. Why not rather follow the way of the Son of Man, the way of submission and service, and thus ensure the establishment of the kingdom of God?

Jesus did not just take part in formal teaching and debate in the temple precincts during these visits to Jerusalem. People

were interested in the presence of this young prophet from
Galilee, whose approach to many religious questions was
so free from subservience to tradition, and they came
to him with a variety of problems, to see what he would
say – and sometimes, it appears, to involve him in some
embarrassment.

One of the chief theological points at issue between the
Pharisees and the Sadducees concerned the doctrine of personal resurrection. The Pharisees had maintained this doctrine since the emergence of their party in the latter half of the
second century BC; the Sadducees rejected it as an innova-
tion. When some Sadducees propounded to Jesus the problem of the future marital status of the woman who had been
married to seven brothers in succession, he dismissed their
problem by observing that marriage belongs to this mortal
life, not to the resurrection life of the age to come. Then he
put the doctrine of resurrection on the firmest possible basis
by grounding it in the nature of God. If God, long after
Abraham, Isaac and Jacob were in their graves, could introduce himself to Moses in the words, 'I am the God of
Abraham, and the God of Isaac, and the God of Jacob', this
meant that, for God, the patriarchs were still alive. 'He is not
God of the dead, but of the living' (Mark 12:27).

On another occasion some Pharisees came to him, while he
was teaching in the temple court, with a less speculative
problem. They brought with them a woman who, they said,
had been caught in the act of adultery. (Her companion in
crime had evidently been able to make his escape, leaving her
in the lurch.) Here was the problem. The law of Moses laid it
down that a person found guilty of this offence should be
sentenced to death by stoning, on the testimony of two or
three witnesses. What was Jesus' ruling? Should she be
executed or not?

They probably suspected that he was no advocate of capital
punishment, and if they knew anything of his record in
Galilee they were probably aware that he was readier to
sympathise with people like this woman than to condemn
them. But if he said that she should not be put to death, he

could be charged with arrogating to himself the authority to set aside the law of Moses – or rather, the law of God given through Moses. On the other hand, if he wished to avoid the appearance of countermanding Moses and said that she *should* be put to death, he would impale himself on the other horn of the dilemma. For, since Judaea had become a Roman province in AD 6, the right to carry out the death sentence (except for violations of the sanctity of the temple) had been taken away from the Jewish rulers; it was a right which the Roman governor reserved for himself. If Jesus defied the authority of Moses, he would discredit himself as a religious teacher; if he could be charged with challenging the privilege of the Roman governor, the immediate consequences for him could be drastic indeed. What would he say?

Where a guilty person was to be stoned to death, the Mosaic law directed that the first stones should be thrown by those whose testimony had made the death-sentence possible. Jesus modified this direction. Instead of 'Let the chief witness throw the first stone' he said, 'Let him who is without sin among you be the first to throw a stone at her' (John 8:7); By 'without sin' he may well have meant 'without this kind of sin'. At any rate, having said this he had no need to say anything more. The dilemma was no longer his, but theirs. They quietly slipped away, leaving the woman to receive from the one who was indeed without sin not the sentence of condemnation but the assurance of forgiveness and the command to sin no more.

Last journey to Jerusalem

Jesus was well aware of the risks he ran in coming to Jerusalem and engaging in public activity there. On one occasion in Galilee, when something said or done by himself or his disciples had annoyed Herod Antipas, he was warned by some friendly Pharisees to take evasive action, or Herod would kill him. Jesus did not take their warning over-seriously. He would complete the work he had to do in

Galilee regardless of Herod's threats.[3] It would never do for a prophet to be killed anywhere but in Jerusalem: Jerusalem was the city that killed prophets. Now he was in Jerusalem, and he knew what that might mean for him.

Indeed, when they were on the way to Jerusalem for the last time, he warned his disciples that the suffering of the Son of Man, of which he had told them while they were still in the north, was about to be realised. But they found such language increasingly incredible. In their minds Jerusalem was not the place where prophets were killed; it was the place where kings were crowned. They knew the identity of the true king of Israel; surely, when he reached Jerusalem, he would disclose his identity openly and receive the welcome that was his due. And when he was greeted as Israel's true king, they themselves, as his loyal followers, would receive appropriate recognition.

Some days before the Passover of AD 30 Jesus and his followers came up the Jericho road to Jerusalem to be present in the city for the annual celebration. Passover commemorated the deliverance of the Israelites from Egypt in Moses' day. Jews all over the known world celebrated it, but only in Jerusalem were the Passover lambs killed and eaten, calling to mind the lambs which were killed and eaten in Egypt on the first Passover Eve. The killing of the Passover lambs ranked as a sacrifice, and the only place in the world where sacrifices could be offered, according to current Jewish law, was the temple in Jerusalem.

The road was thronged with pilgrim crowds, and as they approached Bethany, on the other side of the Mount of Olives from Jerusalem, great excitement was unleashed, for people were still talking about a mighty work recently performed there by Jesus when he had called back one Lazarus to life after he had lain in a rock-tomb for three or four days. Near Bethany a donkey was provided for Jesus to ride on, and as he completed the journey to Jerusalem the pilgrims hailed him as the one who would restore the kingship of David and his line. Some of them at least recognised in Jesus' action the fulfilment of a late prophetic oracle in which Jerusalem was called upon to rejoice at the advent of her king who came to her 'humble, and riding on an ass' (Zechariah 9:9). But few of them understood the message that Jesus wished to convey. He was presenting himself to the people of Jerusalem as the agent of God, inviting them to choose the way of peace rather than the way of armed resistance. Had he come mounted on a war-horse, that would have symbolised a call to military action; but in that case the Roman garrison would have intervened quickly and decisively. As it was, what threat was offered by an unarmed man riding on a donkey, surrounded by a crowd of peasants yelling their heads off?

The temple authorities, however, took the matter more seriously. Here was a crowd, they saw, convinced that the day of liberation was at hand, and if their excitement increased beyond control (as could easily happen) they might do something desperate which would bring down the heavy hand of Rome. Jesus' intentions might be entirely peaceful, but they feared that he would be pushed into becoming at least the titular leader of an insurrection. If Roman reprisals fell on him alone, that would be no bad thing; but the danger was that many others, and perhaps the city and temple as a whole, might feel the weight of such reprisals. If Jesus could be isolated and put out of harm's way, that would be best for all concerned; but the chances of taking action against him without stirring up a riot seemed to be slender while the festival was on.

Cleansing of the temple

Their apprehensions were intensified by his 'cleansing of the temple' a day or two later. In the outer court he protested against the commercial activity that went on there, because it was bound to interfere with the proper use of the sacred area. The outer court of the temple was also known as the 'court of the Gentiles' because it was open to Gentile visitors, who were forbidden on pain of death to penetrate into the inner courts. God-fearing Gentiles who wished to worship the God of Abraham in his temple had to do so in the outer court; their presence there helped to fulfil the divine promise through a Hebrew prophet: 'my house shall be called a house of prayer for all peoples' (Isaiah 56:7). But if the outer court was cluttered up with market stalls and the like, there was the less room for Gentiles to worship God. Hence Jesus voiced his protest: 'Is it not written, "My house shall be called a house of prayer for all the nations"? But you have made it a den of robbers' (Mark 11:17). Moreover, like some of the prophets of old who acted their oracles in addition to uttering them, he backed up his oral protest by driving out the merchants and the animals they sold (animals to be used by the worshippers for sacrificial purposes, presumably) and upsetting the tables where money might be exchanged. There was nothing wrong in itself with such traffic, but his Father's house, he said, was not to be made a bazaar. As the evangelists report the incident, one is reminded of the last sentence in the Old Testament book of Zechariah: speaking of the 'day of the Lord' it says, 'there shall no longer be a trader in the house of the Lord of hosts on that day' (Zechariah 14:21).

This action was in no way directed against the Roman power. The Romans left the administration of the temple in the hands of the Jewish authorities and did not interfere in it. If the action had involved civil disturbance – especially if, as has been suggested, it marked an attempt by Jesus and his followers to take over the temple – the Romans would have intervened at once. Even the temple police, a body of Levites trained to keep order in the sacred precincts, do not appear to have been involved. The protest was a single-handed piece of symbolism on Jesus' part, and the temple authorities seem to have recognised this, for instead of arresting him they asked him by what authority he did it. His reply was more or less to the effect that, if they could not recognise genuine prophetic authority when they met it, no amount of evidence or argument would help. So they left it at that.[4]

Tribute to Caesar

When Judaea became a Roman province in AD 6, its people
were required, as a matter of course, to pay taxes to the
imperial exchequer in Rome, and a census was held to assess
the amount of taxation to be levied on the new province. The
census sparked off a revolt, led by one Judas who was not
himself a Judaean by birth – he came from Gamala in
Gaulanitis (the Golan heights). He and his followers maintained that it was high treason against the God of Israel for his
people to pay taxes, drawn from the produce of the holy land,
to a non-Jewish ruler. This 'fourth philosophy' (as Josephus
calls it) was a completely new doctrine.[5] Judaea had been
tributary to a succession of foreign empires for over four
centuries, from the time of Nebuchadnezzar to the Macca-
baean wars, and no prophet or other religious leader had ever
suggested that there was anything improper about this. On
the contrary, the prophets had taught that it was by God's
providence or judgment that his people found themselves
under foreign domination, so that any attempt to withhold
tribute from their foreign overlords, or otherwise revolt
against them, was opposition to the will of God.

New as Judas's doctrine was, it was nevertheless popular.
The payment of taxes was in any case an unwelcome burden,
and when the people were told that the payment of taxes to
this particular ruler was irreligious, they were disposed to
believe it. Judas's revolt was crushed, but the spirit of revolt
lived on. In due course Judas's heirs formed the party of the
Zealots, which in general accepted the teaching of the Pharisees but added to it Judas's distinctive doctrine about the
impiety of paying tribute to Caesar. It was the Zealots who
played a dominant part in the revolt against Rome of AD 66,
which led to the destruction of the temple and city of Jerusalem four years later. But during the sixty years from AD 6 to
66 (apart from the three years AD 41–44 when Judaea was
ruled by a member of the Herod family, appointed by the
Roman emperor) the question of the propriety of paying
tribute to Caesar remained a sensitive issue.

The Galilaeans, governed as they were by a Jewish tetrarch, were not directly involved in this issue. But when Jesus
came to Jerusalem and began teaching in the temple court, it
was inevitable that he should be faced with the question. A
teacher of such independent mind was likely to say something
original. So he was approached and asked, 'Is it in accordance
with divine law to pay tribute to Caesar? Yes or no?'

The form in which the question was phrased might have
presented many a teacher with a dilemma. If he said 'Yes', he
would forfeit much popular good will; if he said 'No', he could
be charged with fomenting sedition. Jesus asked to be shown
a sample of the money with which the imperial tribute was
paid, and someone produced a Roman coin, a silver *denarius*.
'Whose face is this?' he asked. 'Whose name is here?'
'Caesar's' was the answer. 'Then', said he, 'give Caesar back
what belongs to Caesar; give God what belongs to God'
(Mark 12:13–17).

To one whose total concern was the kingdom of God and
his interests in the world, the question of which ruler received
material tribute was one of minor importance. He urged his
hearers to seek God's kingdom and righteousness, and if they
made that their aim in life, paying Caesar back in his own coin
(literally) would not affect it one way or the other.

Jesus had no exaggerated esteem for rulers as such,
whether for the tetrarch in Galilee, the chief-priestly establishment in Jerusalem, the governor of Judaea or his master in
Rome. To him they were all fallible human beings, occupying
their positions by God's permission and responsible to him for
their conduct. He saw the rich irony of the desire shown by
some rulers in the Near Eastern world of that time for the
honorific title Euergetes, which means 'Benefactor' (Luke
22:25). Such a title ought properly to be given to those who
rendered service to others; it was strange that it should be
sought by those who thought themselves entitled to receive
service *from* others.

There might have been the further implication that those
who used a coin bearing Caesar's likeness stamped on it were
deficient in their loyalty to the God of their fathers, whose law

forbade 'graven images'. Rabbinical tradition knows of certain Jews who paid such scrupulous heed to this prohibition that they refused even to look at a coin which bore an image. But if this implication is present in Jesus' words, it is not expressed and need not be laboured. Money was something of supreme unimportance in Jesus' eyes; it became important only when it was so eagerly sought after that it became an idol.[6] If Caesar demanded money, he was demanding something of no great value in itself; let him have it (especially when it was money which proclaimed itself to be already his). What God required was something infinitely more important: let them see to it that God was not deprived of what belonged to *him*. Jesus not only avoided the dilemma, but turned it so as to emphasise the basic theme of his ministry. Caesar's just requirements are limited; God requires nothing less than all that his people have – and are. A time was to come, later in the first century, when Caesar demanded from Jesus' followers that which was due to God alone, and they appreciated the main thrust of their master's teaching clearly enough to say 'No' to Caesar.

Those who hoped that Jesus' reply to their question would provide material for a charge of seditious speech must have been disappointed. On the other hand, his reply gave little comfort to any whose hopes of an early declaration of independence had been raised by the circumstances of his entry into Jerusalem. If Jesus commanded much less popular enthusiasm at the end of his last week in Jerusalem than at the beginning, his reply to the question about paying tribute to Caesar could explain this.

All this time, however, the authorities had been considering the best way of forestalling the public disorder to which they feared Jesus' teaching and activity in Jerusalem might give rise, especially when so many pilgrims were congregating in the city. An opportunity of taking quiet but effective action to silence him presented itself when one of the twelve, from motives which can only be guessed at, offered to enable them to arrest him when no inconvenient crowd was around.

Chapter 9

Jesus' Last Meals

Table-fellowship in Jesus' ministry

From the time of Jesus' rejection by many of his former followers in Galilee, his words about the immediate future stress the inevitability of the suffering of the Son of Man. This note is intensified as he and his disciples take the road to Jerusalem. Yet the reader of the Gospels nowhere gets the impression that Jesus regarded himself as the victim of an inexorable fate. In word and deed throughout Holy Week he remains master of the situation. He knows what is going on around him; in particular, he is well aware of the plans of the chief-priestly authorities. The time will come when they will have their way with him; however, that time is not under their control, but God's.

Fellowship meals of various kinds had been a feature of Jesus' ministry. He treated them as a parable of the communal joy to be experienced in the kingdom of God. Indeed, the same motif entered into some of his spoken parables – the parable of the great supper, for example, which the first invited guests failed to attend, so that their places had to be filled by the flotsam and jetsam of society; or the parable of the prodigal son, whose homecoming was celebrated with feasting and merriment. Jesus' sitting at table with tax-collectors and outcasts caused scandal to godly souls in Capernaum and its neighbourhood, but it was an eloquent proclamation of God's attitude to sinners. His feeding of the five thousand in the wilderness east of the lake is related by

Mark in a way which makes the reader feel that there is some
deeper significance beneath the surface; John brings out this
deeper significance by reporting Jesus' synagogue address on
the true bread of life.[1]

During the closing days in and around Jerusalem Jesus took
part in two meals to which the narrators attach special importance. At one of these he was an honoured guest; at the other
he himself presided.

Supper at Bethany

The former of the two was held in Bethany, a few days before
the Passover. Mark says it was held in the house of Simon the
leper, of whom we have no other information. Perhaps he had
been cured of his leprosy but continued to be called 'the leper'
by use and wont, to distinguish him from many other bearers
of the name 'Simon'. At any rate, during the meal a woman
emptied a whole flask of very costly perfume over Jesus' head
– an act which provoked indignation on the part of some who
were there, because the perfume was worth nearly a year's
wages for a working man, and the proceeds could have gone
to feed the poor, instead of being thus 'wasted', as they
thought. Jesus, however, accepted the woman's action as an
anticipation of the anointing which his body would normally
receive at its burial. There might be no opportunity to anoint
him then, so she had taken this opportunity. It is not clear
whether this was the idea behind her action or simply Jesus'
defence of her lavish gesture.[2]

John, in narrating the incident, adds some details: he says
that the woman was Mary of Bethany, the sister of Martha
and Lazarus, and that the indignation was voiced by Judas
Iscariot. This Judas was the member of the twelve who went
to the chief priests with an offer to enable them to lay hands
on Jesus, and Mark reports his doing so immediately after his
account of this meal in Bethany. While Jesus accepted the
anointing as an anticipation of his burial, there may have been
some people present who took the woman's action to mean

that she was anointing him as Messiah. In the eyes of such people, she had anointed him king as deliberately as, in Hebrew history, the prophet Samuel had anointed his great ancestor David; and Jesus had accepted and defended her action. Did Judas conclude that his master had allowed himself to be carried away by those who wished to exploit him for political ends? Was he afraid that, if news of the incident came to the ears of the authorities (as it was bound to do), there would be trouble not only for Jesus but for his associates? As has been said, Judas's motive can only be guessed at, but this is one suggestion that has been made.[3] From the evangelists' point of view, however, it was by way of consecration for sacrifice that Jesus was anointed.

The last supper

The other meal which belongs to the record of Holy Week took place on the Thursday evening, on the eve of Jesus' death. Mark and the other synoptic evangelists narrate it as though it were the Passover celebration; John, however, says expressly that it was held 'before the feast of the Passover' (John 13:1). The explanation seems to be that the meal was indeed held as a Passover celebration, but it was held twenty-four hours earlier than the time fixed by the temple calendar. There is evidence for different ways of reckoning the festivals in Israel (including the Passover) around this time; either Jesus and his disciples on this occasion celebrated the Passover according to another reckoning than that of the temple calendar, or else Jesus deliberately arranged to celebrate it with his disciples on the Thursday evening because he knew that he would no longer be alive to celebrate it on the Friday evening. If the Friday evening was the time for the official celebration and they held the feast on the Thursday evening, then they must have held it without the lamb, for the Passover lambs would have been killed in the temple on the Friday afternoon. But the eating of the Passover meal without the lamb was not unprecedented; it was indeed the rule rather than the exception, for the Passover had to be celebrated without the lamb by every Jewish family in the world outside Jerusalem. In none of the New Testament reports of the last supper is there any mention of a lamb being on the table, although nothing can be built on this silence.[4]

Jesus and his disciples constituted a family for the purpose of the Passover meal, and Jesus filled the role of head of the family, reciting the words prescribed for the head of the family on that occasion. The Passover commemorated the great deliverance accomplished by God for his people Israel at the beginning of their national history: it was part of the responsibility of the head of the family to remind the others, at salient points, of features in the story of that deliverance. For example, he explained the main elements of the meal: the unleavened bread betokened the fact that the Israelites left Egypt in such haste that there was no time to wait for the dough to be leavened; the bitter herbs were a reminder of the bitter life they had led under Egyptian oppression, and so on. Before the explanation of the individual elements, a more general formula was recited: 'Behold the bread of affliction which our fathers ate when they came out of the land of Egypt: if anyone is hungry, let him come and eat.' When the bread was actually about to be eaten, the head of the family said the customary grace: 'Blessed art thou, O Lord our God, King of the universe, who bringest forth bread from the earth.' It was at this point that Jesus, having pronounced a blessing over the bread (presumably in these terms), broke it and gave it to his disciples with the words: 'Take it; this is my body.' The bread, which had one meaning for the participants in the Passover meal, was henceforth given a new meaning for the followers of Jesus. His words and action instituted the Christian meal which is variously called the Breaking of Bread, the Holy Communion, the Lord's Supper or the Eucharist.

The Holy Communion

The institution of the Christian meal is recorded in all three synoptic Gospels. Matthew follows Mark fairly closely; Luke has features of his own. There is no record of the institution in John, but something of its inner significance comes out in Jesus' discourse on the bread of life in John 6:32–58.[5] We have, however, an independent account of the institution in the New Testament, set down in writing about ten years before the earliest Gospel was published. This is the account which Paul included in a letter sent to the church of Corinth about AD 55. But Paul was not telling the Corinthian Christians something they did not know before: he was reminding them of something he had given them by word of mouth when he first visited their city and planted their church five years earlier. His account, moreover, goes back beyond that: it was something that he himself had 'received' earlier, probably soon after his conversion, when he shared the Christian meal with a group of believers in Jesus for the first time.

There are differences between Mark's form of the words of institution and Paul's: Paul's form is fuller than Mark's, including some interpretative material. Thus, where Mark reports Jesus as saying, 'Take it; this is my body' (Mark 14:22), when he gave his disciples the bread, Paul reports him as saying, 'This is my body, which is for you. Do this in remembrance of me' (1 Corinthians 11:24). The fact that Paul's account is earlier does not mean that Mark's is less primitive or less accurate. They probably reproduced the form of words handed down in the churches with which they were associated. If today we compare service-books produced by different denominations we shall probably find similar variations in wording; if we attend the communion service in different churches we shall probably hear such variations when the words of institution are repeated. But the basic statement 'This is my body' is constant; whatever is added is designed to bring out its meaning.

When the Passover meal proper was ended and concluding words of thanksgiving had been said, the head of the family took one of the cups of wine from the table and said, 'Blessed art thou, O Lord our God, who createst the fruit of the vine.' Then they all drank. At this point Jesus took a cup and, after blessing God for it in these terms, gave it to his disciples. As they drank, he said, 'This is my covenant blood, which is poured out for many. Truly, I tell you, I shall not drink again of the fruit of the vine until that day when I drink it new in the kingdom of God' (Mark 14:24,25). That is Mark's account. Paul says that when he took the cup 'after supper' he said, 'This cup is the new covenant in my blood. Do this, as often as you drink it, in remembrance of me' (1 Corinthians 11:25). Paul does not reproduce Jesus' words about his next drinking 'the fruit of the vine' in the kingdom of God; he does add words of his own which emphasise a forward-looking aspect to the whole occasion: 'For as often as you eat this bread and drink the cup, you proclaim the Lord's death until he comes' (1 Corinthians 11:26).

If we had only the threefold account in the Gospels, it might not have been immediately clear to us that the special taking of the bread and the cup by the disciples was urged on them by Jesus not for that one occasion only, but was intended to be repeated. However, we might infer this intention from Luke's version, where, on giving them the bread, Jesus says, 'Do this in remembrance of me' or 'Do this as my memorial' (Luke 22:19). These words do appear to point forward to the future; it is not natural to think of a memorial for someone who is alive and very actively present.

In any case, it is certain that from the earliest days of the Christian church this twofold command of Jesus was understood as something requiring the repeated obedience of his followers until his advent in glory; and so it is still understood in almost all areas of the worldwide church. His followers celebrate this feast as his memorial, not simply in the sense that they call him to mind with special intensity but in the sense that their crucified and ever-living Lord comes and makes his presence real to them as they eat and drink.

Jesus' death anticipated

The record of the last supper deserves detailed attention because Jesus' actions and words on that occasion throw light on the significance which he attached to his impending death. That it was impending he had no doubt. He knew of the plans being laid by the authorities; he knew that there was a traitor in the inner circle of the twelve. But he regarded it as of the highest importance that he should share this Passover meal with his disciples before his death. He carefully arranged for the place where it was to be held and took steps to make sure that the traitor should not discover its location in advance. He did not mean to be interrupted and arrested until he had finished preparing his disciples for what lay immediately ahead.

When Jesus said to them, as he gave them the bread, 'This is my body', he may have meant 'This is myself'. 'Body' was one of the nouns used in his language to convey the force of the emphatic English suffix '-self' attached to a pronoun. He intended them to grasp the fact that he was giving them himself, that he was sacrificing himself for them.

When he said, as he gave them the cup, 'This is my covenant blood' or 'This is my blood of the covenant', he used phraseology which would have reminded some of them of its Old Testament background. After the departure from Egypt, when God gave the ten commandments to his people Israel, he brought them into a covenant relation with himself: he undertook to be their God and they undertook to be his people. They would worship no other deity and the law they had just received formed the basic constitution of the covenant. Then Moses took the blood of sacrificed animals and sprinkled some of it on the sacrificial altar (a token of the presence of the invisible God) and the rest of it on the people, saying, 'Behold the blood of the covenant which the Lord has made with you in accordance with all these words' (Exodus 24:8). The covenant ceremony was followed by a meal: the leaders of the people, it is said, 'beheld God, and ate and drank' (Exodus 24:11).

The covenant-blood of which Jesus spoke was his own; it is difficult to avoid the conclusion that he looked on his death as inaugurating a new covenant to take the place of that established in Moses' day. Midway between Moses and Jesus, the prophet Jeremiah foretold how, in days to come, God would establish a new covenant with his people – a better and more durable covenant than that established when the Israelites came out of Egypt (Jeremiah 31:31–34). Some later New Testament writers had no doubt that it was through Jesus that this promise of a new covenant was fulfilled; and indeed Paul and Luke, in their report of the words of institution spoken over the cup, say 'new covenant' where Mark (followed by Matthew) has simply 'covenant'. The implication is that Jesus had in mind the establishment of the new covenant foretold by Jeremiah. This at least is certain: through the death of Jesus (which is what is meant by the outpouring of his blood) men and women have been brought into a new and abiding relation with God. When they drink the communion wine, they acknowledge with gratitude this relation into which Jesus, through his death, has introduced them.

Moreover, according to Mark, Jesus spoke of his blood as being poured out 'for many'. This phrase has the same force as it has in his saying that the Son of Man came 'to give his life as a ransom for many' (Mark 10:45); in both places it probably envisages the extension of the saving benefits of his death to embrace Gentiles as well as Jews. To Mark's phrase 'for many' Matthew adds the interpretative words 'for the forgiveness of sins' (Matthew 26:28).

Jesus was to be violently seized and put to death. But he was not content to be a passive and protesting victim: he would take the initiative and, in the hour of death, present his life to God as a sin-offering for others. The idea of presenting one's life to God in this way was not unprecedented. Some of those faithful Jews who were put to death for refusing to forswear their faith in the days of the Maccabees are recorded as offering up their sufferings to God on behalf of their fellow-Israelites. One of them, the aged scribe Eleazar, said with his last breath, 'O God, . . . be gracious to thy people, and let our punishment be a satisfaction for them. Make my blood their purification, and take my life to ransom theirs' (4 Maccabees 6:27–29). Similar efficacy on Israel's behalf is ascribed in some strands of rabbinical theology to the self-surrender of the patriarch Isaac, when his father Abraham was about to sacrifice him on Mount Moriah. (Isaac's life, however, was spared at the last moment.)[6] But it is a matter of historical fact that, within a generation of the death of Jesus, many men and women from Israel and the Gentiles alike experienced the liberating assurance of forgiveness of sins through his death, not to speak of the many more who have experienced the same assurance in each succeeding generation since then. The giving up of his life has indeed proved to be 'a ransom for many'.

When Jesus said, after giving his disciples the cup, 'I shall not drink again of the fruit of the vine until that day when I drink it new in the kingdom of God', he meant this at least: the final establishment of the kingdom of God which he had proclaimed – the rule of God in the lives of human beings – was to be dependent on his death. His death was to be more powerfully effective than any preceding aspect of his ministry. Neither he himself in prospect, nor his disciples in retrospect, regarded his death as an abrupt termination to his ministry, but rather as the event which crowned his ministry.

Chapter
10

Arrest and Trial

Arrest in the garden

After keeping the last supper with his disciples, Jesus left the
upper room where it had been held and went with them to a
spot on the western slope of the Mount of Olives, across the
Kidron ravine, where he had been in the habit of going
with them. Judas knew that he would be going there, and
slipped out of the upper room before the others, in order to
lead the temple police to the place where they could arrest
him.

There has been a tendency in recent times to ascribe the
initiative in the final action against Jesus exclusively to the
Roman authorities in Judaea. This has been in part a reaction
against the monstrous calumny which has branded the whole
Jewish nation of that day, and indeed of succeeding days, with
responsibility for Jesus' death. Not only is this calumny
lacking in any historical foundation; it bespeaks an appalling
insensitivity towards Jesus' own people on the part of those
who have claimed to be his followers. It must indeed be
emphasised that Jesus was sentenced to death by a Roman
judge and executed by Roman soldiers. Everyone knows
this, of course; but what people 'know' as a matter of
course does not necessarily affect inherited attitudes or
prejudices.

On the other hand, the testimony of the New Testament
writers ascribes the initiative to the temple authorities, and
this is confirmed by the earliest Jewish references to the trial

and execution of Jesus.[1] This cannot be explained entirely in terms of a desire to exonerate the Roman administration from responsibility in the matter.

It is not unthinkable that the Jewish authorities should have handed over an inconvenient religious teacher for the Romans to deal with. 'Violent reactions by the Jewish religious authorities towards one of their subjects', says Dr Geza Vermes, 'and their handing over of him to the jurisdiction of the Romans, do not necessarily imply that in their judgment a religious or political crime has *actually* been committed. The offence may simply have been irresponsible behaviour *likely* to lead to popular unrest.'[2] He points to the case of another Jesus, the son of one Ananias, who at the Festival of Tabernacles in AD 62 began to fill Jerusalem with his prophecies of woe against the temple and the people. Unable to silence him, the Jewish authorities handed him over to the Romans. By doing so, they avoided being charged with failure to do their duty, and freed themselves of the necessity of dealing further with an embarrassing situation – embarrassing, because many people thought the man was a genuine prophet. The Roman governor had him flogged and then let him go.[3]

The spot to which Judas led the men who were sent to arrest Jesus bore the name Gethsemane ('the olive press'). Its exact location cannot be ascertained, but it cannot have been far from the place to which that name has been traditionally attached. Mark (followed by the other synoptic evangelists) tells how, before the arresting party arrived, Jesus was heard praying in intense agony of spirit that he might be spared the approaching ordeal (that the 'cup' might pass him by); if it could not be otherwise, however, he submitted himself to his Father's will. In the prayer which he had earlier taught his disciples to use, the petition 'Thy kingdom come' was interpreted to mean 'Thy will be done'. What he had told them about the kingdom of God was incarnated in himself when he prayed in Gethsemane, 'yet not what I will, but what thou wilt' (Mark 14:36) – and acted accordingly. Two hundred years later the Alexandrian Christian leader Origen coined a

Greek word (*autobasileia*) to designate Jesus as 'the kingdom in person'.[4] It was an inspired coinage.

The men whom Judas led to the place where they could arrest Jesus were members of the temple police, who were under the authority of the captain of the temple and his chief-priestly associates. But John says quite explicitly that they were accompanied by Roman troops – the 'cohort' that was stationed in the Antonia fortress (or at least a substantial part of that cohort), under the leadership of their commanding officer, the 'military tribune' (John 18:3,12). Yet these Roman soldiers did not play a leading part in the arrest. Perhaps the Jewish authorities were afraid that Jesus might be attended by a body of men prepared to offer armed resistance, on a scale with which the temple police could not cope, and had arranged for the presence of the Roman soldiers lest there should be such resistance. As it was, however, their assistance was not required.

Chief-priestly inquiry

The Gospels represent Jesus as having been brought before a Jewish court and then before the Roman governor, Pontius Pilate. For his appearance before the Jewish court we are indebted mainly to Mark (who is followed by Matthew and Luke). His appearance before the Roman governor is recorded by all four evangelists, but the most coherent account of it is given by John. John says nothing about his appearance before a Jewish court, although he does report a preliminary inquiry held in the house of Annas, the senior ex-high priest.[5] This inquiry, which is not mentioned in any of the other Gospels, tried to investigate more fully the nature of Jesus' teaching and the identity of his disciples. Jesus replied that his teaching was a matter of public knowledge: he had nothing to add to what he had openly taught in the temple precincts. So he was sent bound, under police escort, from the house of Annas to the headquarters of Caiaphas, Annas's son-in-law, the reigning high priest.

It is disputed whether Jesus appeared before the Sanhedrin, the supreme court of the Jewish nation, convened in its regular judicial capacity, or before a court of inquiry. In either case, the high priest presided, and the court consisted of members of the Sanhedrin – 'chief priests, elders and scribes' (Mark 14:53). But even when the Sanhedrin met as a formal court of law, the execution of a death-sentence was at present beyond its competence: this was something which, in keeping with general Roman usage, the provincial governor reserved to himself.[6]

As a concession to Jewish religious sentiment, however, there was one area in which the Roman administration allowed the Sanhedrin to exercise unrestricted authority: this was the area of offences against the sanctity of the temple. Here, no doubt, we have the explanation for the statement in Mark's account that, when the court had been convened on this occasion, some witnesses affirmed that Jesus had been heard to say, 'I will destroy this temple that is made with hands, and in three days I will build another, not made with hands' (Mark 14:58). That was the general purport of their testimony, but they did not agree in their detailed wording, and the strict Jewish rules of evidence ruled their allegations out of court. If their evidence had been admissible, there would have been a prima facie case for the court to go ahead and deal with the charge on its own authority, without any reference to the Roman governor.

Nothing that Mark has recorded earlier in his Gospel prepares the reader for this charge. He does indeed say that, a few days before, Jesus had told his disciples that of the great buildings which made up the temple complex not one stone would be left standing on another; it would all be demolished (Mark 13:2). This was to take place forty years later, but nothing was said at that time of any rebuilding of the temple. John, however, throws light on the foundation for the charge when he tells how Jesus, challenged about his authority to 'cleanse' the temple, replied, 'Destroy this temple, and in three days I will raise it up' (John 2:19). John, in the light of Jesus' rising from the dead, explains that he was speaking of 'the temple of his body'. One might think also of the 'temple not made with hands' to which Paul and other New Testament writers refer, using the words as a figure of speech for the new community of Jesus' followers. Whatever it was that Jesus precisely said, it stuck in people's memories, for one of the taunts hurled at him when he was on the cross was 'Aha! You who would destroy the temple and build it in three days, save yourself, and come down from the cross!' (Mark 15:29,30).

However, the attempt to convict him of a threat to the temple proved unsuccessful. No other witnesses were forthcoming at short notice, and yet it was expedient (as the high priest had decided) to have Jesus put out of harm's way as quickly as possible, for once the news of his arrest got around, there was the danger of a popular demonstration. So, with doubtful legality, Jesus was put in a position where he was liable to incriminate himself. 'Are you the Messiah, the Son of the Blessed One?' the high priest asked him. If he had answered this question with a simple 'Yes', he could not have been charged with a religious offence: there is no reason to suppose that a claim to be the Messiah was in itself a breach of Jewish law, even when it could not be substantiated. But such a claim had political implications which could expose anyone who made it to a charge of sedition in Roman law. For, by general consent, the title Messiah was equivalent to 'King of the Jews' – and sovereignty over the Jewish nation belonged at this time to the Roman emperor. 'Every one who makes himself a king sets himself against Caesar' (John 19:12); there could be no doubt about it.

Jesus knew that, however he answered the high priest's question, he would incriminate himself in relation either to Jewish law or to Roman law, if not in relation to both. He made sure, therefore, that the record should be set straight and that the indictment should be framed in his own terms. If 'Messiah' was the word the high priest and the other judges chose, well and good. It was their word, not his; but if they insisted on it, he could not deny that he did claim to be the Messiah. But if he were to choose his own form of words, let them take knowledge that from now on they would 'see the

Son of Man seated at the right hand of the Almighty, and coming with the clouds of heaven' (Mark 14:62).

The judges could scarcely believe their ears. The accused man, they reckoned, had convicted himself out of his own mouth. No need of further witnesses: this was plain blasphemy, and they had heard it for themselves. In later codifications of Jewish law, blasphemy was limited to the pronouncement of the unutterable name of the God of Israel (the name spelt with the four consonants YHWH). There is no suggestion that Jesus pronounced this name, but his language, to those who grasped its purport, implied that he was the assessor and peer of the Most High. If this did not amount to constructive blasphemy, it is difficult to imagine what did count as such. If Jesus had contented himself with claiming to be the Messiah, the Pharisaic members of the court might have deplored his claim but they would not have regarded it as ground for a severe sentence and they would probably not have been happy about handing him over to the Romans. But his additional words altered the situation. It was not safe for the city or the nation to let such a 'blasphemer' go free; God would not hold them guiltless if they took no steps to restrain him.

In looking at Jesus' use of the designation 'the Son of Man', we have considered its relation to Daniel's vision in which he saw a human figure, 'one like a son of man', coming 'with the clouds of heaven' before the Ancient of Days to be vested with universal dominion and to take his seat beside him. The reference to Daniel's vision in Jesus' reply to the high priest's question cannot be missed. It was not unnatural to link Daniel's language with that of the oracle of Psalm 110:1 where an unnamed person, identified by Jesus and his contemporaries as the Messiah, is invited to sit at God's right hand until his enemies are subdued beneath his feet. It is the oracle of Psalm 110:1 that is echoed in Jesus' description of the Son of Man 'seated at the right hand of the Almighty'.

Whatever the reaction of Jesus' judges was to these words of his, their astounding implications should not be lost on us. Condemned and discredited by earthly courts, Jesus is about to be vindicated in the heavenly court. Henceforth, he will be recognised as God's agent in blessing and in judgment. It is difficult to dismiss his words, so far as their present setting is concerned, as Mark's creation in the light of the church's later faith in Jesus' exaltation. Essentially the same claim, in less pictorial terms, is made by Jesus in other gospel strands, both before his passion and after his resurrection. 'All things have been delivered to me by my Father' (Luke 10:22); 'All authority in heaven and on earth has been given to me' (Matthew 28:18). But only by his humiliation and crucifixion was this claim made good; for him the way of suffering was the way of glory, and the same was to be true for his followers also. But there was to be little enough of glory seen during the hours that lay ahead.

Jesus before Pilate

The hearing before the Jewish court took place, exception-ally, by night; this was necessary if the process was to be completed before the official Passover. Besides, if it should prove necessary (as it did) to refer the case to the Roman governor, it had to be borne in mind that a Roman official began the day's business at about 6 a.m., and liked to get it over by 10 a.m. Pilate had probably been advised by the chief-priestly party that they would probably be bringing a convicted person before him for sentence early in the morn-ing. Pilate would not be greatly interested in the charge of blasphemy (capital offence though it was in Jewish reckon-ing), but he could not overlook the charge of sedition. Since Jesus had virtually claimed to be king of the Jews, Pilate (it was hoped) would simply rubber-stamp the decision of the high priest and his colleagues that Jesus had committed a capital offence, and order the death sentence to be carried out.

Instead, Pilate surprised them by formally opening a fresh trial and asking them, as prosecutors, to state their charge against Jesus. Pilate's right to conduct the case as he thought fit was unquestioned: subject to the overriding authority of Roman law, a governor had complete discretion within his own province. When the chief priests protested that they had already judged the man to be a criminal, he told them to inflict the appropriate punishment that their own law prescribed. They protested again that they were unable to do this, because their law prescribed the death penalty for the offence that had been committed, and this they were prevented by Roman law from executing. But, seeing that Pilate was virtually opening a fresh trial, they framed their charge against Jesus in terms of which Pilate would take immediate cognisance: they charged him with claiming to be king of the Jews, and were ready to testify that they had heard him make this claim in their presence.

Pilate accordingly turned to Jesus and invited him to reply to the charge: 'Are you the king of the Jews?' he asked. Of all four evangelists, it is John who follows most closely here the regular procedure of a Roman trial, combining (after his fashion) historical accuracy with theological interpretation. He provides theological interpretation at this point by transposing Jesus' reply to Pilate's question in such a way as to bring out the true nature of Jesus' kingship.

Jesus, in fact, is represented by John as doing before Pilate something of the same kind as Mark says he did before the high priest. He does not repudiate the term 'king' as totally inadmissible, just as he did not repudiate the high priest's word 'Messiah' – 'but if you are talking of kings and kingdoms', he added in effect, 'the kingdom with which I am concerned is the kingdom of truth, and my subjects are those who love the truth' (John 18:33–38). As C. H. Dodd put it, to the first readers of John's Gospel, sixty years after the event, it was a matter of purely academic interest who was or who was not king of the Jews in AD 30, but the question where ultimate truth is to be found can never cease to be of moment to people who take life seriously.[7] Pilate may or may not have been interested in such questions (more probably not), but they had nothing to do with the matter in hand, he reckoned, so he dismissed the subject with an impatient 'What is truth?'

Jesus, to his way of thinking, was a harmless lunatic, not the stuff of which rebels were made. If he were flogged and then dismissed with a caution, that would meet the situation.

Before any further action was taken, however, the question of the customary release of a prisoner at Passovertide was raised. There is no unambiguous reference to this customary release anywhere outside the New Testament; within the New Testament all four evangelists mention it. In particular, both Mark and John mention it; this means that we have two independent lines of evidence for it.[8] The custom was, we are told, that the governor released at Passover any single prisoner for whom the people asked. Possibly this was a custom taken over by the Roman governors from previous rulers of Judaea; probably it was intended to commemorate the release of the people's ancestors from their servitude in Egypt. We do not know. On this occasion Pilate hoped that they might ask for Jesus' release; he was taken by surprise when the crowd of bystanders shouted, 'Not him; we want Barabbas!' Barabbas really was the stuff of which rebels were made; he had recently been seized after participating in an insurgent outbreak in which blood had been shed. But plainly he was regarded as a popular hero, a bold freedom-fighter; his release was therefore sought – and granted. The insurgent was set free; the preacher of peace and non-resistance was convicted of insurgency. The irony of the situation is brought out by the evangelists; it was probably not lost on Pilate himself.

Jesus, then, was handed over to the soldiers for a flogging. They improved the occasion by dressing him up in mock coronation robes and pretending to pay him homage, in ridicule of his alleged claim to be king of the Jews. John tells how Pilate then presented him, dressed up as he was, to the chief priests in expectation that they would be satisfied that Jesus offered no more threat to anyone. But they resented Pilate's scarcely veiled hint that this sorry figure was a worthy king of them and their nation, and they refused to give up pressing their charge. For a moment, however, they changed the terms of the charge. If Pilate did not take seriously Jesus'

alleged claim to be king of the Jews, they insisted that the
terms in which he claimed to be the Son of God amounted to a
serious offence in Jewish law, deserving the death-sentence;
they demanded that Pilate should exercise his authority by
directing that the death-sentence be carried out. But, after a
further brief interrogation of Jesus, Pilate showed himself
equally unwilling to satisfy them on that score either.

Then they played their last card. 'Never mind about the
charge of blasphemy, then,' they said in effect; 'come back to
the charge of sedition. Anyone who claims to be a king in one
of the imperial provinces infringes Caesar's authority; if you
release this man you are no friend of Caesar's' (John 19:12).
On at least one occasion since his arrival as governor Pilate's
tactlessness (not to use a harsher word) had caused the Jewish
authorities to send a complaint about him to Rome, and the
complaint had been treated seriously. But no complaint
would be treated so seriously as a report that he had dis-
charged a man who, as the chief priests would testify, had
been guilty of seditious language. The Emperor Tiberius was
a notoriously suspicious character, and such a report would
not go down at all well with him. Pilate's mind was made up
for him, and he pronounced the death-sentence.

John describes in detail the time and place of the passing of
the death-sentence. It was towards noon on Friday of Passover Week, he says (the trial had taken longer than expected). The raised platform or *tribunal* had been set up in the
courtyard of Government House (the *praetorium*), in an area
called the Pavement or the Plainstones. Pilate sat down in his
chair of office on the platform and sentenced Jesus to death by
crucifixion.

Secular and spiritual authority

John dramatises the confrontation, as to some extent the
other evangelists also do. Here are two forms of authority.
Pilate is vested with secular authority, the authority of the
world-ruler whose lieutenant he is – he has armed force at his

disposal, adequate to carry out his commands. Jesus represents a kingdom 'not of this world' – the authority at his disposal is that of the Father who has sent him into the world. What can such authority avail against Roman military might? To outward appearance it can avail nothing: Jesus is seized and led off to the place of execution. But the evangelists, by the time they came to tell their story, knew better. Jesus' authority was asserted in his submission to injustice, brutality and death; and it was his authority, not Pilate's, that was vindicated in the event. Even Pilate's authority, and the imperial power from which it was derived, could be exercised only by the permission of God; and in this instance the exercise of Pilate's authority was overruled for the furtherance of God's saving purpose in the world. Pilate sat in the judge's chair and Jesus stood condemned before him; but the evangelists knew (in common with other Christians) that Jesus is the divinely appointed judge of the living and the dead, and that it was really Pilate, and Jesus' chief-priestly accusers, who were on trial before *him*. But that is not how it appeared at the time.

Chapter 11

The Crucified King

The way to the cross

From Pilate's headquarters Jesus was led off to the place of execution, outside the north gate of Jerusalem, by the roadside. Crucifixion was intended to be a deterrent to others as well as a punishment for the convicted person, so the more public it was the better. Two other men were crucified with him. They are described as 'bandits', which was a term commonly applied to those activists who would nowadays be called terrorists or freedom-fighters, according to the speaker's viewpoint. Possibly they were associates of Barabbas in a recent outbreak of insurgency.

The traditional site of the death of Jesus, within the precincts of the Church of the Holy Sepulchre, is probably authentic. But the traditional route to the cross, the Via Dolorosa, leading from the Ecce Homo Arch to the Holy Sepulchre, is a matter of debate. It is probably accurate enough, if Pilate had his headquarters at the Antonia fortress (where today stands the Convent of our Lady of Zion); there are, however, weighty arguments in favour of the view that his headquarters (on his occasional visits to Jerusalem) were in Herod's palace, on the west wall of the city (where the Citadel stands today by the Jaffa Gate).[1]

The place of execution, for some reason which can only be guessed at, was called 'The Skull'. The two names by which it is most familiarly known to us, Golgotha and Calvary, represent the Aramaic and Latin words for 'skull' respectively.

Here, then, Jesus was crucified. It was customary for a man condemned to the cross to carry his cross, or at least the cross-bar, on his shoulders to the place of execution; this is the background of Jesus' words to his disciples about taking up one's cross to follow him. The Roman soldiers who took Jesus to the place of execution commandeered the services of one Simon, a man from Cyrene, who was on his way into the city through the north gate, to carry Jesus' cross (or cross-bar) for him. Simon's family was well known in the church in the next generation: when Mark, relating the incident for the benefit (probably) of Roman Christians about AD 65, wishes to identify Simon for them, he says (in effect), 'You will know which Simon I mean if I tell you that he was the father of Alexander and Rufus' (Mark 15:21).

The work of crucifixion was carried out by a squad of Roman soldiers. John mentions four soldiers (a quaternion), but it is not clear if the four carried out all three crucifixions, or if four men were detailed to see to each separate crucifixion. When they had completed their task (which was all in the day's work for them), they sat down to keep guard, in case any attempt might be made by the men's friends to rescue them.

The death of the cross

Crucifixion – the fastening of a human body to a tree, a stake, a plank or the like – might take a variety of forms, all of them hideous. In ancient Israel the body of an executed criminal (the execution having been carried out, for example, by stoning) might be hung up on a tree or a gibbet, but the law directed that it should be taken down at sunset and buried out of sight, because the spectacle was an affront to God: 'a hanged man is accursed by God; you shall not defile your land which the Lord your God gives you' (Deuteronomy 21:23). But when we speak of crucifixion, we usually think of it as a means of executing a living person. If even the public exposure of a corpse was recognised as offensive to God, who created humanity in his own image, it was vastly more offensive so to treat a living body. There are forms of execution which are not reckoned to strip a person of every vestige of dignity, but crucifixion was designed to do just that.

Crucifixion seems to have been introduced to the Mediterranean world from the east. Assyrian bas-reliefs showing the siege and storming of enemy cities depict citizens being impaled outside the walls. A good example is provided by the depiction of the siege of Lachish on a wall of Sennacherib's palace at Nineveh. Crucifixion in the stricter sense was practised by the Persians: when Darius I put down a rebellion at Babylon, for example, he is said to have crucified 3,000 Babylonians. Alexander the Great took over some of the worse as well as some of the better aspects of the Persian way of life: when the people of Tyre resisted him on his southward march towards Egypt and held up his progress for seven months, he took his revenge not only by destroying their city but also by crucifying 2,000 of them along the seashore.

The barbarity of the Hasmonaean king Alexander Jannaeus (103–76 BC) reached its climax when, having put down a revolt among his subjects, he crucified 800 of them conveniently near his palace so that he and his friends could watch them from a balcony. As a further refinement, he had their wives and children butchered before their eyes as they hung on the crosses. 'Truly an unlovely man, though he was High Priest and King.'[2] His action is mentioned with horror by a Qumran commentator on the prophecy of Nahum: this 'hanging men up alive', he says, 'was never before done in Israel'. (He means that it had never before been done by an Israelite; it had been done *to* Israelites by Antiochus Epiphanes.) Herod the Great could be ferocious enough in his punitive actions, but he is never said to have crucified anyone.

It was the Romans who introduced crucifixion as a routine means of execution into the land of Israel. They may originally have taken the practice over from Carthage (which was a Phoenician colony). Among the Romans it was the form of capital punishment reserved for slaves. Slaves had no legal or official dignity, and so could not be deprived of any. Roman citizens were specifically exempt from such a degrading penalty. When Rome extended its rule further afield, crucifixion was used as the appropriate penalty for non-Romans who were found guilty of rebellion or sedition. When the Roman general Quinctilius Varus put down a rebellion in Palestine after Herod's death in 4 BC, he crucified 2,000 of its ringleaders.[3] When Jesus, who was not a Roman citizen but belonged to one of those 'lesser breeds without the law', was convicted of sedition, it followed inevitably that he would be sentenced to death by crucifixion.

Crucifixion was not only a prolonged and unspeakably painful method of execution; it was also utterly humiliating. A crucified man was exposed naked to the jeers and abuse of the populace like one who was fastened in the stocks or the pillory; there was, however, eventual release from the stocks or the pillory, but none from the cross. The victim was already racked with pain from the flogging and general rough treatment before he was fastened to the cross; then, with the agony, the cramp, the dehydration, the flies, the stench, he endured a living death for hours or even days. The provision of a projecting support or seat from the upright stake was designed not to give him some relief but to prolong his ordeal. The weight of the body fixed the thoracic cage so that the lungs could not expel the inhaled air, but the leverage afforded by this wooden support made it possible for breathing by diaphragmatic action to continue for a long time.

The victim might be fastened to the cross by ropes or by nails. The synoptic evangelists do not indicate which method was used in Jesus' case, but John says explicitly that nails were used. The use of nails is illustrated by the discovery in 1968 of an ossuary or bone-container on Ammunition Hill, north of Jerusalem. This ossuary proved to contain the bones of a young man (John the son of Ezekiel by name) who had been crucified in the early part of the first century AD. He had been fastened to the cross with three nails – one through each forearm just above the wrist and a third through both heels together. (Not only so, but his legs had been broken as also, according to John, were the legs of the two men who were crucified along with Jesus.)[4]

The charge on which Jesus was condemned to death was displayed on a placard attached to the cross: proclaiming him to be 'king of the Jews', it was worded in such a way as to give deliberate offence to the Jewish leaders. Here, it was implied, was a king worthy of such a nation. Neither Pilate nor the leaders of the nation could have envisaged a time, not far distant, when many would recognise that Jesus did in fact reign from the cross – that the crucified one was the kingliest king of all.

The cross: the climax of divine revelation

Three of the evangelists introduce features in their accounts of the crucifixion which help to relieve its horror. Luke tells how one of the bandits crucified alongside Jesus acknowledged his kingship and received the assurance of a place with him in paradise; John tells how Jesus from the cross committed his mother to the care of the beloved disciple; Matthew records natural and supernatural phenomena – rending rocks and opening tombs. But Mark tells the story in unrelieved grimness right to the moment of Jesus' death. In his account Jesus' last articulate words are 'My God, my God, why hast thou forsaken me?' But as soon as he has told how Jesus breathed his last he adds two pieces of information which set the scene in a new perspective. 'The curtain of the temple', he says, 'was torn in two, from top to bottom. And when the centurion, who stood facing him, saw that he thus breathed his last, he said, "Truly this man was the Son of God!"' (Mark 15:38,39).

No explanation is offered of the tearing of the temple curtain. We cannot even be sure if Mark is referring to a literal curtain in the temple at Jerusalem, or is speaking figuratively. If a literal curtain is intended, it is nevertheless the figurative significance that is important. Literal or figurative, the curtain

in mind is probably that which hung across the entrance to the
inner sanctuary, the holy of holies, barring the way into it
from the outer sanctuary, the holy place. The inner sanctuary
was empty; it was the throne-room of the invisible God of
Israel. Only one person was permitted to pass through the
curtain. That was the high priest, and even he did so on one
day in the year only, on the Day of Atonement, when he
presented sacrificial blood to make atonement first for his
own sins, and then for the sins of the nation which he
represented in the sight of God. The whole structure, like the
ritual which was enacted there, emphasised the remoteness of
God and the difficulty of gaining access to him, dwelling as he
did in deep darkness. Happily, there were Israelites who
knew the joy of coming near to God in spiritual experience,[5]
quite apart from the ritual of approaching him in the temple;
but so far as the ritual was concerned, access to his presence
was severely restricted. But with the death of Christ, says
Mark, the curtain has been torn as though by an almighty
hand – 'from top to bottom' – and the way to God stands wide
open so that whosoever will may come. God is no longer
concealed in deep darkness; he is fully revealed in the death of
Christ.

Job, in his day, spoke of the revelation of God to be seen in
the works of creation: 'Lo, these are but the outskirts of his
ways; and how small a whisper do we hear of him! But the
thunder of his power who can understand?' (Job 26:14). Now,
however, in the death of Christ may be seen not merely 'the
outskirts of his ways'; his very heart is bared. It is no faint
whisper but the 'thunder of his power' that sounds from the
cross, and it sounds in accents of redeeming grace: 'Lo, this is
our God, we have waited for him . . . let us be glad and
rejoice in his salvation' (Isaiah 25:9).

The torn curtain, in fact, has much the same significance
as the centurion's words. The centurion was the non-
commissioned officer in charge of the soldiers on guard at the
place of execution. What this pagan could have meant by
saying, 'this man was the Son of God', is uncertain – probably
something like 'this man was divine'. The earlier editions of

the Revised Standard Version translated the words, 'this man was a son of God'; and this no doubt comes close enough to what he meant.[6] But Mark discerns a deeper meaning in his words, a meaning which is at one with the truth he wishes to emphasise in his whole record. The translation preferred in the later editions of the Revised Standard Version expresses Mark's intention: 'this man was the Son of God'. At the beginning of Jesus' earthly ministry, according to Mark, Jesus' identity was attested by the heavenly voice: 'You are my beloved Son' (Mark 1:11). It is attested in similar terms by the voice from the cloud which three of the disciples heard on the mountain of transfiguration: 'This is my beloved Son' (Mark 9:7). And now at the end it is confirmed in the spontaneous utterance of the most unlikely person present at the cross. It is on the cross, in his humiliation, helplessness, dereliction and death, that Jesus is most clearly seen as the Son of God – that is to say, in this context, as the perfect revelation of God. John, in his Gospel, explores more fully what is implied in Jesus' identity as the Son of the Father, but essentially John's doctrine of the person of Christ is not higher than Mark's. John writes as a spokesman of those who can say of the Son of God, 'we have beheld his glory' (John 1:14); but even for John it is in the death of Christ that the glory of God shines most brightly.

The preaching of the cross

In those days the cross, as an instrument of execution, was not to be mentioned in polite society. The Latin word (*crux*) was, in more senses than one, a four-letter word. The first preachers of the gospel had a formidable handicap to overcome when they began to proclaim the crucified Jesus as the Saviour of the world. To cultured Greek ears the idea was disgusting and utterly absurd. For Roman ears it had, in addition, sinister implications. The fact that Jesus had been crucified, by the sentence of a Roman judge, meant that he had been convicted of sedition; was it not probable that those who acknowledged themselves to be his followers were guilty at least by association? As for Jewish hearers, the statement in the law of Moses that a hanged man was an offence in the sight of God was understood to mean that the divine curse rested on him, by the very fact of his being hanged. The claim that a crucified man, a hanged man, was the Messiah of Israel was a blasphemous contradiction in terms. The Messiah was one on whom, almost by definition, the divine blessing rested in a unique degree; how then could he be recognised in one who had died the death on which the curse of God was explicitly pronounced?

There was every reason in the world for the disciples to play down the circumstances of their master's death. But they did nothing of the kind; they pushed the cross into the forefront of their preaching. One notable preacher of the apostolic age, Paul of Tarsus, declared that he would glory in nothing else than 'the cross of our Lord Jesus Christ' (Galatians 6:14). Such a declaration is the more remarkable because it came from a man who earlier had been most conscious of the impossibility (as he reckoned) of imagining that one who died under the curse of God could be what his first disciples claimed him to be. But he learned, first in his own inner life and then in his experience as a preacher of the gospel to others, that the message of Christ crucified embodies the power and wisdom of God, because it proved more effective in the reclamation of men and women than all the schools of Greek philosophy.

This effectiveness has persisted throughout the centuries. There is a redemptive power in Christ crucified unmatched anywhere else. Many, from all parts of the world, have said of him what Bunyan's pilgrim said: 'He hath given me rest by his sorrow, and life by his death.'[7]

Chapter
12

The Risen Lord

Burial

So far as the Romans were concerned, the bodies of crucified criminals might be left hanging for several days after death, as a warning to others. But in Judaea the Roman administration paid some respect to Jewish religious susceptibilities. By Jewish law it was not proper that corpses should be left hanging after sunset, and that was specially important when (as on this occasion) the next day was the sabbath. The Jewish authorities therefore made representations to Pilate, who gave orders for the bodies of the three men to be taken down from their crosses. The legs of the two 'bandits' were broken to hasten death; but by this time Jesus was already dead. One of the soldiers, says John, pushed a spear into his side just to make sure. John saw conformity with ancient prophecy both in the negative fact that Jesus' legs were not broken and in the positive fact that his side was pierced.[1]

The bodies might be unceremoniously disposed of, but if the family or friends of an executed person requested leave to bury the body, the request would normally be granted. Leave of this kind had evidently been given to the friends of John the son of Ezekiel, the crucified man whose ossuary was discovered in 1968.[2] In the case of Jesus, it was not a member of his family or one of his close followers who secured his body for burial, but a member of the Sanhedrin, Joseph of Arimathaea. He was a sympathiser with Jesus' message of the kingdom of God, and plucked up courage to approach Pilate and ask for Jesus' body. He had a plot of ground quite near the place of execution, and when his request was granted he took the body and placed it in a rock-tomb hollowed out in that plot. Time was pressing, for the sabbath would start at sunset, and nothing more could be done till the Sunday morning.

The empty tomb

Early on the Sunday morning Mary Magdalene and some other women, who had followed Jesus and his disciples from Galilee to Jerusalem, came to the tomb to pay their last respects to his body (since there had been no opportunity of doing so on the Friday evening). To their dismay, they found it empty, and concluded (naturally) that the body had already been moved.

When Christians affirm their belief in the resurrection of Christ, they are not referring primarily to the fact that his tomb was found empty. They are referring to the fact that, on that first day of the week, Jesus appeared to several of his disciples alive again – alive not merely for a further brief spell but alive for evermore.

The early Christians did not believe that Jesus was risen again because they could not find his dead body. They believed because they had found the living Christ. When they first began to proclaim Jesus in public as the risen Lord, they did not say, 'We found his tomb empty', but 'We saw him alive.' But the terms in which they made their proclamation *implied* that the tomb was empty.

When a tomb has been opened and found to be empty, the obvious assumption to make is either that a body was never placed there or else that it has been removed. When the tomb of Jesus was found to be empty, it was assumed that the latter had occurred. Mary Magdalene wept as she said, 'They have taken away my Lord, and I do not know where they have laid him' (John 20:13). She thought that someone – the gardener, perhaps – might have removed it, and she asked where it was in order that she might arrange to give it permanent and decent burial. The last idea to occur to her was that Jesus had come to life and left the tomb. Even when he spoke to her, she did not at first think it was Jesus.

There was no point, then, in proclaiming that the tomb was empty; that could be explained very simply. But empty it certainly was, whatever the explanation might be. When the fact that it was empty became a matter of widespread knowledge, those authorities who had no wish to let the disciples' preaching of the resurrection have its way unchallenged put the story about that the disciples came to the tomb during the night and stole the body while the guards, who should have prevented them, were sleeping.[3] If it be asked why a more convincing story was not put about, the answer is probably that the authorities, being more familiar with the relevant circumstances than we can be at this late date, knew what they could get away with.

What is meant by resurrection?

The apostolic proclamation was: 'Jesus is alive.' But if he was alive, it followed that he could not be in the tomb.

It is easy for us today to talk of a spiritual resurrection and emphasise that this is what is really important. What does it matter if 'John Brown's body lies a-mouldering in the grave' so long as 'his soul goes marching on'? But that is not what the followers of Jesus meant when they spoke of his resurrection in the first century AD, and that is not what their hearers understood them to mean. By 'resurrection' they meant the resurrection of the body; if they had meant only that the spirit and power of Jesus lived on, 'resurrection' is not the word they would have used. (They might have spoken rather of 'a sort of immortality' or said that, though dead, he still empowered others.)

Moreover, even if they had used this word to mean that Jesus' spirit and power lived on, their proclamation would have been pointless if his body was still in the tomb, or in some other place to which it had been moved. The authorities would simply have organised visits to the place to demonstrate that he had not risen from the dead, in the only sense which those words carried for most Jews at that time. Christianity would never have got off the ground. Indeed, if Jesus had not risen from the dead, we should probably never have heard of him.

Not more than twenty years after Jesus' death, Paul of Tarsus visited Corinth and preached the gospel there. He based his message on three historical facts, as he believed them to be – facts which he held in common with men who had been around at the time in question. They were these: Christ died; Christ was buried; Christ was raised on the third day. (This mention of 'the third day' was constant in the early apostolic preaching and is enshrined in the church's creeds; it implies inclusive reckoning in which the three days are Friday, Saturday and Sunday.) The fact that Christ was buried receives separate mention, not only to emphasise that he was really dead ('dead and buried', as we say, to emphasise the reality and finality of the death), but also to indicate that the resurrection was a reversal not only of the death but also of the burial – in other words, to indicate that Jesus left the tomb untenanted.

Paul, for his part, had never seen the empty tomb; he became a Christian when he met the living Christ on the Damascus road. But some of those who met the living Christ at an earlier date, on the third day from his crucifixion, also saw the empty tomb. One of these has left a circumstantial record of what he saw.

That is the record preserved in John 20:1–10. The historical tradition which forms the basis of the fourth Gospel bears the signs of first-hand testimony, and that is true of this part of John's resurrection narrative. Writing as a dramatic critic, the late Dorothy L. Sayers pointed out that the fourth Gospel 'is the only one that claims to be the direct report of an eyewitness', and she added, 'and to any one accustomed to the imaginative handling of documents, the internal evidence bears out this claim.'[4] There is certainly something of an eye-witness quality about John's description of the empty tomb, and especially of the arrangement of the grave-clothes which had been left behind – an arrangement which suddenly made the beloved disciple realise what had happened: 'he saw and believed' (John 20:8).

The early preaching

In the earliest Christian writings that have been preserved for us, the resurrection of Jesus is presupposed and affirmed. If (as I am disposed to believe) the earliest Christian document surviving is Paul's letter to the Galatians, written about AD 48, then it opens with Paul's introduction of himself as an apostle 'through Jesus Christ and God the Father, who raised him from the dead'. If (as most New Testament students think) the earliest Christian document is the first letter to the Thessalonians, sent by Paul and two of his colleagues to the church of Thessalonica in AD 50, the recipients of that letter are reminded at an early stage how they 'turned to God from idols, to serve a living and true God, and to wait for his Son from heaven, whom he raised from the dead' (1 Thessalonians 1:9,10). It is plain from such references that what is there set down in black and white was earlier proclaimed by word of mouth.

Both these documents come from Paul (whether in association with others or not), but the resurrection message did not originate with Paul. Paul accepted it for himself about AD 33, when the risen Lord appeared to him on the Damascus road and conscripted him into his service; but Paul knew that others were proclaiming it before that event. However, it is to Paul that we owe the earliest summary of Jesus' resurrection appearances. He gives it in 1 Corinthians 15:1–8. That letter (as we have seen in another connection) was written in AD 55. But in this passage Paul reminds the Christians in Corinth of something that he told them when he first preached the gospel in their city, five years previously. In addition, what he told them then was something that he himself had been told several years before that, quite early in his Christian career.

According to Paul's own account, when he first came to Corinth he decided, in preaching to those who lived there, to 'know nothing' among them 'except Jesus Christ and him crucified' (1 Corinthians 2:2). This was because he knew that the proclamation of a crucified Saviour would make no concessions to those standards of secular wisdom by which the Greeks of Corinth and elsewhere set so much store; rather, it made nonsense of them. But it is plain from the whole tenor of Paul's writings that for him the proclamation of Christ crucified involved the proclamation of Christ risen from the dead. Paul knew, before his conversion, that Jesus had been crucified; that had simply convinced him that Jesus could not be the Messiah of Israel. It was the revelation of the crucified Jesus *risen from the dead* that turned Paul round in his tracks and made a Christian of him. The crucifixion and the resurrection are necessary to each other. There can be no gospel without both, for neither is meaningful without the other.

The resurrection appearances

Paul in fact, as we have seen, emphasised in his preaching to the Corinthians the three historical facts of Christ's death, his burial, and his resurrection on the third day. When he reminds them how he told them that Christ 'was raised on the third day in accordance with the scriptures', he reminds them further how he told them

> that he appeared to Cephas, then to the twelve. Then he appeared to more than five hundred brethren at one time, most of whom are still alive, though some have fallen asleep. Then he appeared to James, then to all the apostles. Last of all . . . he appeared also to me.

Paul says that this summary of resurrection appearances, which he 'delivered' to the Corinthians, had previously been 'received' by himself. It was not necessary for Paul that anyone should 'deliver' to him the assurance that the Christ who died was alive again; that assurance came to him directly when he personally saw the risen Christ. The statement, 'Last of all . . . he appeared also to me' (1 Corinthians 15:8), is Paul's own contribution to the summary of resurrection appearances. But that it was on the third day that Christ was raised, and that he appeared in resurrection to 'Cephas' (that is, Peter), James and others – all this Paul 'received' from those who could speak from their own experience, and especially from Peter and James when he met them in Jerusalem about AD 35, in the third year after his conversion. At that time, as Paul says in his letter to the Galatians, he spent two weeks with Peter. This was his first personal contact with any of the leaders of the Jerusalem church. The only other leader of the church whom he met during that visit was James – James the brother of Jesus, who was to play a prominent part in the life of the Jerusalem church until his illegal execution in AD 62. It would be only natural for Peter and James to tell Paul how the risen Lord had appeared to them, as he told them how the same Lord had more recently appeared to him.

Peter was the leading apostle: it is not surprising that the risen Lord should appear to him. Another reference to that appearance is given in Luke 24:34: when the two Emmaus disciples to whom the risen Lord revealed himself on the evening of Easter Day walked back to Jerusalem to break the glad news to their friends, they found the apostles and others full of the same news: 'The Lord has risen indeed', they were saying; 'he has appeared to Simon' (meaning Simon Peter).

But the appearance to James is more surprising. James, and with him the other members of Jesus' family, were less than enthusiastic in their attitude to him during his ministry. Perhaps they foresaw where his activity was leading him, and his crucifixion confirmed their worst apprehensions. Yet from the earliest days of the church the brothers of Jesus are seen in a leading role, and especially James. What caused their earlier lack of sympathy to give way to ardent espousal of their brother's cause when, by all natural reckoning, it proved to be a disastrously lost cause? Just this: in resurrection 'he appeared to James'.

When Paul says repeatedly that the risen Christ 'appeared' to this one and that, including himself, he places the experiences of those others on a level with his own. He does not mean that their experiences were as 'visionary' as his; he means that his was as real and objective as theirs. By saying that Christ 'appeared' to them, rather than that they 'saw' him, he implies that the initiative lay with Christ: he let himself be seen by them. Paul has no objection to saying that he saw the risen Christ – 'Have I not seen Jesus our Lord?' he asks indignantly when doubt is cast on his apostolic status (1 Corinthians 9:1) – but in the public proclamation emphasis was laid on Christ as the one who was active throughout.

Faith and fact

It is important to distinguish between the resurrection faith and the resurrection fact. The resurrection faith – the belief that was awakened in the followers of Jesus that he had risen from the dead – is itself generally recognised to be a historical fact. But it is not to be confused with the resurrection fact – the fact that Jesus actually came alive after his death and burial, never to die again. The resurrection of Jesus was not on a level with the temporary restoration to life of others who had been dead for shorter or longer periods, like Jairus's daughter or Lazarus of Bethany. What they experienced was a renewal of mortal life; in due course that mortal life was conclusively terminated by death. But the disciples never imagined that this was what had happened to their master. His resurrection life, they understood, was a new order of existence; it was an anticipation of that 'life of the age to come' which many Jews of that time expected to follow the resurrection of the last day.

The resurrection faith depends on the resurrection fact; otherwise it is empty. 'If Christ has not been raised', said Paul to the Corinthians – if there was no resurrection fact – then 'your faith is vain' (1 Corinthians 15:14,17). The resurrection fact must have a character commensurate with the quality and effect of the resurrection faith. The resurrection faith demands an adequate cause. One view that has commended itself to some scholars recently is that the resurrection faith was born in the mind of Peter, in 'a conversion experienced in the form of a vision'[5] or 'a moment of truth bringing intellectual certainty'.[6] But while Peter certainly did undergo such an experience, to identify this experience with the resurrection fact itself is to place on it a weight which it is unable to bear. The experience of James, when the risen Christ appeared to him too, was most probably independent of Peter's, as Paul's later experience certainly was. The experiences of all three – the devoted, though temporarily defeated, disciple; the unsympathetic brother; the determined persecutor – share a common cause. In all three the resurrection faith was independently kindled, and kindled by one and the same resurrection fact: Jesus, who was crucified, was no longer dead, but alive. This is the resurrection fact which the New Testament offers us to match the resurrection faith.

There are those (and I am one of them) whose instinctive response to others who have difficulty in accepting this basic New Testament presentation is to ask, as Paul did before the younger Agrippa, 'Why is it thought incredible by any of you that God raises the dead?' (Acts 26:8). But it has to be realised that the intellectual climate of western culture since the seventeenth or eighteenth century has not been congenial to the idea of the miraculous. Where a non-miraculous explanation is adequate, it is natural to prefer it. But what non-miraculous explanation is adequate to account for the resurrection fact and faith together, along with their lasting effects? Paul, I believe, was right in viewing the resurrection of Christ from the dead as the supreme manifestation of God's power. Here, in C. S. Lewis's terminology, we have a miracle of the new creation;[7] more than that, we have *the* miracle by which the new creation has been brought into being.

The role of the women

According to the resurrection accounts in the Gospels, it was
not to Peter or to any other of the male disciples that the risen
Lord first appeared; it was to women, and primarily to Mary
Magdalene. The appearance to Mary Magdalene is vividly
described in the fourth Gospel. C. H. Dodd, discussing this
description, speaks of his 'feeling' (cautiously he adds, 'it can
be no more than a feeling') that it 'has something indefinably
first-hand about it. It stands in any case alone. There is
nothing quite like it in the gospels. Is there anything quite like
it in all ancient literature?'[8]

I cannot agree with those who view the accounts of Jesus'
appearance to Mary Magdalene and the other women with
greater scepticism than the accounts of his appearance to
Peter and the other male disciples. His appearance to the
women is not likely to have been invented. For one thing,
the women are made to play a much more creditable part in the
passion and resurrection narratives than that played by the
male disciples; for another thing, those who preserved the
accounts of Jesus' appearance to the women would have
known that they were inviting disbelief in the whole resurrection message. The testimony of women, especially with
regard to a matter of this kind, would simply be discounted as
not to be taken seriously. According to Luke, when Mary
Magdalene and her companions told the male disciples what
they had seen and heard at the empty tomb, 'these words
seemed to them an idle tale, and they did not believe them'
(Luke 24:11); still less would they have believed them if they
had reported that they had seen the Lord himself. In later
generations the involvement of women in the gospel accounts
of the resurrection was regarded as sufficient reason for
dismissing the whole idea out of hand. Celsus, a second-
century polemicist against Christianity, regarded the belief in
the resurrection as based on nothing more than the halluci-
nation of a 'hysterical female'.[9] Here is a sufficient reason for
the silence about Jesus' appearance to the women in the early
apostolic preaching. What Paul gives us in 1 Corinthians

15:3–11 is a summary of that preaching as he had 'received' it and as he 'delivered' it to others in turn. No specific mention was made in it of the testimony of women. But when we consider the practical reasons against making any mention of it, the historicity of the tradition that Mary Magdalene was the first person to see the risen Lord is not put in question by its absence from the public proclamation.

Time and manner

The resurrection appearances took place over a period of some weeks both in Jerusalem or its vicinity and in Galilee. It is perhaps possible to arrange them in a chronological pattern which bears some relation to the sacred calendar of Israel at that time of year.[10] Pilgrims who had come from Galilee to Jerusalem for Passover and the ensuing week's Festival of Unleavened Bread would make their way home again after the festival; some of them would return to Jerusalem a few weeks later to be there for the Festival of Pentecost, which fell seven weeks after Passover. This could provide an explanation for the earlier appearances taking place in and around Jerusalem, later ones in Galilee, and the final one near Jerusalem. But there can be no certainty on this score. One thing seems clear: after a few weeks the appearances came to a decisive end. The last one ended with Jesus' disappearing from the disciples' view in circumstances which showed them that he had been taken into the presence of God; the cloud which, according to Luke, 'received him out of their sight' (Acts 1:9) is the cloud which enveloped the divine glory.

The appearances did not all take the same form. At times the risen Lord seems to have been recognised instantly; more often he was not recognised, or was mistaken for someone else, until by familiar voice or gesture he made his identity known. But the outcome was to leave the disciples in no doubt that, contrary to the expectation of his friends and enemies alike, the Lord was risen indeed. The resurrection faith came to life in their hearts because of the objective resurrection fact, which took place independently of them and made its inescapable impact on them: Jesus, the crucified one, was brought back from death and appeared to them as the living one, alive for evermore.

The 'hinge' event

It is the resurrection event that forms the hinge between the Jesus of history and the Christ of faith. There is no clear-cut frontier between the two, as though one should say that it was the Jesus of history who was crucified and the Christ of faith who rose again. Christ crucified is a historical figure, indeed, but Christ crucified is very much the object of his people's faith. Christ risen is also the object of his people's faith (for Christ crucified and Christ risen are not two Christs, but one), but Christ risen is, at the same time, a figure of history. If nothing intervened between Jesus' burial and the disciples' conviction that he had been raised from the dead, the historian would be left with a credibility gap. As a pure historian, he might be content to say that something happened after Jesus' death and burial sufficient to account for the rise of the resurrection faith, without committing himself on the precise nature of that 'something'. Where historical research can go no farther, the primitive Christian witness affirms that that 'something' was Christ's being raised from death by the power of God.

The disciples recognised the Lord who appeared to them in resurrection as identical with the Lord whom they had known before his death, the Jesus of history; but they quickly became aware that he now belonged to a different order of existence. He became less and less accessible to them as the Jesus of history, and more and more accessible as the Christ of faith. The Christ of faith was indeed 'this same Jesus' as they had seen and heard during his earthly ministry, but he was now withdrawn from them in that earlier form in order to be nearer to them in this new form – nearer not only to them but also to the rapidly increasing number of believers who had never known him in the old form.

Chapter 13

Jesus and the Jewish Parties of His Day

Sadducees

Of all the religious parties in Israel in the days of Jesus, the one with which he had least in common was the Sadducean party. The Sadducees appear to have been drawn from the wealthy landed aristocracy, the old established families. It was they who supported the Hasmonaean dynasty of priest-kings during most of the time that it exercised power.[1] It was from their ranks that, in the period following the collapse of the Hasmonaean dynasty, the high priests and members of the temple establishment came. They belonged to a different social class from the rank and file of ordinary priests, who were of humble status, living by their work on the land when their presence was not required in the temple (the number of priests was so large that, apart from the great festivals, a priest would serve in the temple for one week only in each half-year).

Theologically, the Sadducees followed what they believed to be 'the old-time religion'. They regarded the Pharisees as innovators, with their oral tradition designed to adapt the ancient law to modern conditions; the Pharisees' belief in the resurrection of the body was rejected by the Sadducees as a new doctrine with no biblical foundation. (The one Old Testament document where it is unambiguously taught is the book of Daniel; but the Sadducees quite probably did not accept that book as part of the canon of sacred writings.)

The one occasion on which Jesus is recorded as having encountered the Sadducees on the theological level was when some of them approached him in the temple court during his last week in Jerusalem and presented to him the conundrum about the resurrection which we have mentioned above.[2] Jesus took care to reply to them on the basis of the Pentateuch, the five books of Moses, to which they accorded the highest authority. Some scribes of the Pharisaic party, who were listening in, were so impressed by his reply that they could not withhold their commendation: 'Well spoken, Teacher!' they said (Luke 20:39).

Pharisees

The reader of the Gospels is sometimes surprised to be told that the party with which Jesus had most in common was the Pharisees.[3] How comes it, then, he may ask, that Jesus and the Pharisees appear to have been involved in controversy every time they crossed each other's path? A partial answer to that question is found in the fact of experience that, in religion as in politics, it is often those parties that have most in common that engage most in mutual criticism. Our perspective will be enlarged if we take account of the evidence of the Acts of the Apostles in addition to that of the Gospels. The disciples of Jesus who formed the church of Jerusalem shortly after his death and resurrection met with opposition chiefly from the Sadducees. This is intelligible when we recall that it was the Sadducean chief priests who handed Jesus over to Pilate; they could not be expected to look any more kindly on Jesus' followers. But theologically the Sadducees took sharp exception to the disciples' public preaching because they proclaimed that Jesus had been raised from the dead, in anticipation of the end-time resurrection in which the Sadducees did not believe. But, partly for that very reason, the disciples were tolerated, if not encouraged, by the Pharisees.

Gamaliel, for example, the most influential Pharisee of his day, and the leader of the Pharisaic group in the Sanhedrin, spoke up in the Sanhedrin when the chief priests were minded to take extreme action against the disciples: 'Leave these men alone', he said. 'If their movement is of purely human origin, it will fizzle out and come to nothing. But if it comes from God, you will never be able to overthrow it; you might even be found fighting against God!' (Acts 5:34–39). Gamaliel expressed sound Pharisaic doctrine: the cause of God will win in the end, whatever human beings may do. On this occasion Gamaliel's argument persuaded the majority of his fellow-members of the Sanhedrin.

There was indeed one young Pharisee, a pupil of Gamaliel's, who did not agree with his master in this matter. In his eyes the new movement presented too deadly a threat to Israel's sacred traditions to be left in peace: it must be suppressed, and the sooner the better. But Saul of Tarsus, persecutor-in-chief of the infant church (until his confrontation with the risen Lord on the Damascus road turned him into the leading propagator of the gospel), was far from being a typical Pharisee.

Some members of the Pharisaic party actually joined the early church in Jerusalem. To their existing beliefs they added the belief that Jesus, crucified and now risen from the dead, was the promised Messiah of Israel; their new faith did not oblige them to abandon any essential feature of their Pharisaism. They were foremost among those members of the Jerusalem church who tried to insist that Gentile converts to the new faith should be required to submit to various requirements of the law of Moses; this was probably their means of ensuring that such converts should be weaned from their former pagan ways by having to conform to a firm ethical code. It is interesting that the chief opponent of their policy should be no other than Saul (also called Paul)[4]: as he had in earlier days been a zealot for his ancestral traditions, so after his conversion he showed himself a zealot in the cause of Christian liberty. It was of great importance in his eyes that Gentile converts should lead lives worthy of the Lord whose followers they now were, but submission to the law of Moses was not (as he saw it) the way to achieve that end. Paul had been an exceptional Pharisee before his conversion, and after it he was an exceptional Christian.

But even Paul, in his Christian days, could find himself on the same side of the fence as the Pharisees. During his last visit to Jerusalem he was charged with a serious offence against the sanctity of the temple, and was brought before the Sanhedrin. He began his defence by claiming that the central issue in the controversy in which he was involved with the leaders of the Jewish people was the resurrection: 'it is with regard to the hope of resurrection for the dead that I am on trial' (Acts 23:6). This was not disingenuous: Paul knew from his own experience that Jesus had risen from the dead, and the resurrection of Jesus confirmed the resurrection faith in which he had been brought up. Moreover, the resurrection of Jesus was absolutely crucial to the gospel he proclaimed: as he says in another place, 'if Christ has not been raised, then our preaching is in vain' (1 Corinthians 15:14). But when he expressed himself in these terms before the Sanhedrin, he divided that body into two. The Sadducean majority, of course, rejected his claim out of hand, but the Pharisees argued that a man who was so sound on the resurrection could not be terribly far astray: as for his Damascus-road experience, what if a spirit or an angel had spoken to him? (To the Sadducees, who had no place in their creed for spirits or angels, this was so much nonsense.)

If then Pharisees and Jewish Christians could find common ground in the decades immediately following Jesus' ministry, it would not be surprising if Jesus and the Pharisees found some common ground during his ministry.

But did he not call the Pharisees hypocrites? It is often supposed that he did, to the point where 'Pharisee' and 'hypocrite' have been treated as synonyms. The word 'hypocrite' in Greek is not always a term of disparagement; it means an actor. In religious language, however, it denotes someone who plays a part expected of one who has certain religious convictions, someone who goes through the appropriate motions, without actually having those convictions at heart. In a society which set great store by the punctilious observance of religious obligations, in such matters as food restriction, ceremonial purity, tithing, prayer, fasting and so forth, there would be a temptation for some to gain a reputation for piety by being seen to observe these things, even if they knew nothing of true heart-religion. Serious-minded Jews were well aware of this temptation, and had no high opinion of those who yielded to it. There is a place in the rabbinical writings where seven categories of Pharisee are distinguished – some of them not unlike those which incurred Jesus' censure – and only one receives unqualified commendation: the Pharisee who is a Pharisee for love of God.[5] Jesus for his part criticised those Pharisees who scrupulously paid tithes on every garden herb but neglected 'justice and the love of God' (Luke 11:42). It was those who concentrated on external minutiae at the expense of the things that really mattered whom he described by the word translated 'hypocrites' – that is, actors.

His words that have been rendered 'Woe to you, scribes and Pharisees, hypocrites!' (Matthew 23:13) should rather be translated 'Alas for you, hypocritical scribes and Pharisees!' They were not intended to stigmatise all Pharisees as 'hypocrites' or actors. The form in which they have come down to us in Matthew 23 may reflect a period later in the first century when the lines of division between Jewish Christians and Pharisees were more sharply drawn. But it would be fair to say that the Pharisees whom Jesus criticised most severely were those who were unfaithful to the noblest ideals of Pharisaism. For the Pharisees were among the spiritual heirs of those faithful souls who had faced martyrdom for their religion in the persecution under Antiochus Epiphanes. The noblest ideals of Pharisaism were well maintained in Jesus' day – for example, by Nicodemus, who sought a night interview with Jesus at an early stage in Jesus' ministry and later spoke up in his defence in the Sanhedrin when it was proposed to condemn him unheard.[6]

Even so, the conflict between Jesus and the Pharisees cannot be denied. There were various reasons for his incurring their displeasure. For one thing, his consorting with notorious 'sinners' showed that he had little time for the rules of ceremonial purity, which would have dictated the avoidance of such people. More serious still was his disregard for the sabbath law, as the Pharisees saw it – actually, what he disregarded was their traditional interpretation of the sabbath law, but it was difficult for them to discern this distinction. And when he was taken to task for what seemed to be his laxity in relation to the sabbath, the terms in which he defended himself were most disturbing. He claimed the authority, as the Son of Man, to decide what was and what was not in keeping with the sanctity of the Sabbath, in disregard of the traditional interpretation of the law. David, the future king of Israel, on the run from the hostility of King Saul, was given for himself and his men the holy bread in the sanctuary which the law permitted to be eaten by none except the priests – and Jewish interpreters inferred from the narrative of 1 Samuel 21:1–6 that this took place on the sabbath day. If David's need could override a plain regulation of the law of Israel, Jesus claimed that human need should override the sabbath law. But who was he, the scribes naturally asked, to dispose in this sovereign fashion of the sabbath law and its application? Who gave him the authority to do so?

In the Gospel of John Jesus goes further still in defending his performance of acts of healing on the sabbath day: 'My Father continues to work', he said, 'and so do I' (John 5:17). It could not be denied that God maintained his providential care over his creatures on the sabbath day as on all other days. If he suspended this care on the seventh day, the world would immediately cease to exist, and a new creation out of nothing would have to be undertaken at the beginning of each week. There was indeed some debate among the rabbis on the question as to whether God did or did not keep his own sabbath law, and some ingenious arguments were devised to show that he did, without desisting from his continuous work of providence. These arguments, however, are irrelevant to the point Jesus made according to John's narrative – that, since the Father kept on working on the sabbath, the Son followed his example. This, in the eyes of his critics, was an outrageous thing to say: in speaking thus he crossed the inviolable frontier and trespassed on the province of deity.

The same kind of trespass was involved, according to the synoptic evangelists' account, when Jesus took it upon himself to pronounce the forgiveness of sins. It was not that he assured people (on the ground of their repentance or some other adequate reason) that God had forgiven or would forgive their sins; he pronounced their forgiveness, it appeared, on his own authority. This is why some of the scribes who heard him thought that his language amounted to blasphemy: 'Who can forgive sins but God alone?' they asked (Mark 2:7). In reply, he declared that 'the Son of Man has authority on earth to forgive sins'; but his declaration did nothing to remove the sense of disquiet which they felt.

However much there was in Jesus' ethical teaching and in his resurrection faith that would have commanded the approval of many Pharisees, his evident disregard for the rules of purity and, above all, the sovereign freedom with which he handled the law as a whole, presented a threat to the very foundations of Israel's religious heritage. So, at any rate, it seemed to many who would readily have laid down their lives for the ideals of Pharisaism. Those who appreciate the nobility of the Pharisaic ideals, but consider that Jesus' way was better still, may reflect that the second best is often the worst enemy of the best.

Herodians

On one or two occasions Pharisees and Herodians are represented as making common cause against Jesus. In general, Pharisees and Herodians had nothing in common: if they found themselves united in opposition to Jesus, it must have been a very temporary and opportunistic union. The Herodians were more a political than a religious party. As their name indicates, they existed to maintain the interests of the Herod family. During the ministry of Jesus, two members of that family occupied positions of authority in or near the land of Israel: Herod Antipas was tetrarch of Galilee and Peraea, and his brother Philip was tetrarch of a region east and north-east of the lake of Galilee. The Herodians whom we meet in the Gospels were supporters of Herod Antipas. If a threat arose to his position, it was their business to deal with it. Such a threat seemed to arise during the Galilaean mission of the twelve. The Herodians would naturally see it as their duty to eliminate the threat which, they thought, Jesus and his followers offered to their master's security.

About this time Jesus is said to have put his disciples on their guard against 'the leaven of the Pharisees and the leaven of Herod' (Mark 8:15). They did not grasp his meaning. He referred to forces which were inimical to the kingdom of God; by the 'leaven of Herod' he did not probably imply any theological doctrine, but the political philosophy of the Herodian party. When he was warned to clear out of Galilee because Herod wanted to kill him, he referred to Herod as 'that fox' (Luke 13:32) – one of the rare occasions on which he made a personal reference to someone in authority. In spite of the threats of Herod or the Herodians, however, he felt secure in Galilee: it would never do, he said with some irony, for a prophet to meet his death anywhere but in Jerusalem – and in Jerusalem Herod's writ did not run.

One thing is certain: it has never been suggested that Jesus had any affinity with the Herodians.

Zealots

It is far otherwise when we turn to another influential party in first-century Judaism – the party of the Zealots.[7] It is arguable that no party was distinctively designated thus before AD 66, but that is relatively unimportant. The party of the Zealots perpetuated the philosophy put forward in AD 6 by Judas the Galilaean when he stirred up a rising against the Romans on the occasion when Judaea was annexed as an imperial province. Judas showed himself zealous in the cause of Israel's God, following the tradition of zeal established in earlier days

by Phinehas, Elijah and Mattathias (father of Judas Maccabaeus and his brothers).[8] Indeed, he went further than any
Jewish zealot had ever done before, arguing that it was wrong
for the people of God in the holy land to pay tribute to a
Gentile ruler. This, as we have seen earlier, provides the
background to the question about paying tribute to Caesar
which was put to Jesus in Jerusalem.[9]

Well, it may be said (and indeed rightly so), Jesus was no
Zealot; if he had been a Zealot, or even a Zealot sympathiser,
he would have answered the question about whether it was
right to pay tribute to Caesar with a direct 'No'. Instead, he
told his questioners to give Caesar what Caesar could rightly
claim; but the Zealots would have said that Caesar had no
rights whatsoever in Judaea, nothing that he could rightly
claim.

Moreover, Jesus' most distinctive ethical teaching stressed
the importance of non-retaliation: his followers should turn
the other cheek, repay evil with good, go willingly a second
mile when their services were requisitioned for one. That was
nothing like the policy of the Zealots.

Yes, *but* (it has been argued) this pacifist line probably did
not originate with Jesus himself. The time came, after the
outbreak of the Jewish revolt against Rome in AD 66, when it
was expedient for the church to dissociate itself from anything
in the nature of resistance to the Roman power, and the
teaching of Jesus was edited (by Mark and others) so as to
represent him as urging his followers to suffer injustice and
oppression uncomplainingly and comply cheerfully rather
than grudgingly with the demands of the occupying forces.

But where is the evidence for this? The editing of Jesus'
teaching (it is said) has been very thoroughly carried out, but
here and there we come upon tell-tale traces of an earlier
and different viewpoint from that now represented in the
Gospels. For one thing, it is pointed out, one of the
twelve specially selected disciples was Simon the Zealot.[10]
Yes, but another was Matthew the tax-collector. The word
'zealot' indeed was used as a common noun to denote a
person of zealous temperament; it did not necessarily identify

him as a member of the Zealot party, though granted, the designation was probably given to Simon in a sense that implied more than merely a zealous temperament. However, even if Simon had been associated with a resistance party at one stage, his inclusion among the twelve apostles suggests that he was now as much an *ex*-Zealot as Matthew was now an *ex*-tax-collector.

Attempts have also been made to discern allusions to revolutionary activity in the sobriquets given to Simon Peter (as though Bar-Jonah referred not to his father's name but to his membership of a resistance organisation),[11] to James and John (as though 'sons of thunder' or 'sons of tumult' betokened a spirit of revolt), and to Judas (as though Iscariot referred not to the place from which his family came but to his belonging to the *sicarii* or 'dagger-men' who, some twenty years after the time of Jesus, embarked on a policy of assassinating pro-Roman members of the Jewish community). But none of these attempts has been successful.

Another piece of evidence, found in Luke's account of Jesus' conversation with his disciples at the last supper, has been invoked to support the Zealot line. Jesus reminded them that when he sent them out two by two to proclaim the message of the kingdom of God, they went without supplies for the journey, because they could rely on the generosity of well-wishers in one place after another. But now, when he himself was to suffer as a criminal, they would be counted as outlaws and could no longer expect to find sympathisers, so they would have to take supplies wherever they went – and a sword as well, he added. 'Look, Lord', they said, 'here are two swords' – to which he replied 'it is enough' and dropped the subject (Luke 22:35–38).

Here, one writer has said, Luke 'records an incident that Mark might well have deemed it politic to suppress, namely, that Jesus took the precaution of seeing that his disciples were armed before going to Gethsemane'.[12] But it was not the arrest in Gethsemane that Jesus had in mind, but the situation in which his disciples might find themselves after he was taken from them. His reference to the sword was ironical: if they

were to be outlaws, they might as well play the part properly.
He dropped the subject when they took him with serious-
minded literalness. Two swords would be ludicrously insuf-
ficient against the armed band that effected the arrest in
Gethsemane, let alone the powerful opposition that they
would have to meet in days to come. When one of the two
swords was actually used in Gethsemane, Jesus sternly told its
bearer to put it back in its sheath.

But Jesus was actually executed by the Roman authorities
on a charge of sedition, was he not? Yes; the inscription on
the cross, 'The King of the Jews', makes that quite clear.
What lay behind that charge? A careful reading of the Gospel
narrative shows that 'The King of the Jews' was the expedient
translation, into terms of which the Roman governor was
bound to take cognisance, of Jesus' claim to be the Messiah –
even if, in the very voicing of that claim, he actually used
words which emphasised its non-political character.

The 'tell-tale traces' which are alleged to point to a Jesus
with Zealot, anti-Roman, sympathies do not in fact point that
way at all. A Zealot sympathiser can be reconstructed only by
removing the hard evidence which we have in the Gospel texts
and replacing it not with evidence of another kind but with
imagination.

The replacement of a resistant activist by the pacifist Jesus
of the Gospels cannot be laid at Mark's door, earliest of the
evangelists though he was.[13] Much of the relevant material in
the Gospels bears the label 'Q' in literary criticism: that is to
say, it belongs to a collection of sayings of Jesus made
probably in the fifties of the first century for use in the rapidly
expanding Gentile mission, long before the Jewish revolt
against Rome is supposed to have dictated a radical reshaping
of the public image of the Jesus preached by the early
Christians into the image presented by Mark.

The picture of the Zealot Jesus was originally the product
of academic speculation. The so-called 'quest of the historical
Jesus' is commonly held to have started with Hermann
Samuel Reimarus, whose study of the aim of Jesus and his
disciples, posthumously published at Brunswick in 1778,

argued that Jesus, like John the Baptist before him, was a revolutionary. One of the most fascinating statements of this thesis (though in many respects an exasperatingly wrong-headed one) is presented in Robert Eisler's *The Messiah Jesus and John the Baptist* (1931) – the English edition of a longer German work in two volumes, 'Jesus the King who did not Reign' (published in 1929 and 1930). Eisler's argument was based largely on his eccentric interpretation of certain passages in the medieval Old Russian version of Josephus's *History of the Jewish War* which are absent from the Greek text. This was a very shaky foundation on which to build, but Eisler, who was a man of gigantic erudition but indifferent judgment, had a very persuasive way of presenting an argument.

A much more moderate interpreter of Jesus as a Zealot sympathiser was Professor S. G. F. Brandon, who held the Chair of Comparative Religion in the University of Manchester from 1951 to 1971. His *Jesus and the Zealots* was published by Manchester University Press in 1967. It was a serious and scholarly work, calling for a reasoned reply. Such a reply was prepared by a group of scholars (most of whom were associated with the University of Cambridge), but a series of untimely delays held up its publication until 1984, when it was issued by Cambridge University Press as *Jesus and the Politics of His Day* (edited by E. Bammel and C. F. D. Moule). Long before that date Professor Brandon himself had died, and the thesis for which he had argued had more or less died with him – so far, at least, as its academic defence was concerned.

But at the non-academic level the picture of a revolutionary Jesus has made a powerful appeal. Revolutionary theologians and leaders of resistance movements have eagerly invoked the authority of such a Jesus to justify recourse to violent rebellion on the part of the oppressed against their oppressors. The late Professor Brandon, who was a man of conservative temperament (for all his radical theology), was rather dismayed to find his scholarly conclusions taken up eagerly for non-scholarly ends by Black Panthers and others whom he could not regard as natural allies.

There is nothing unworthy or ignoble in resistance by the oppressed against their oppressors. Nations which have won their liberation from foreign overlords tend to regard their struggle for independence as the noblest chapter in their history. But one thing has to be said: the authority of the historical Jesus cannot be invoked for such a struggle, whether by a subjugated nation or by an oppressed social group. He taught that violence was no answer to violence. His own nation, directly (as in Judaea) or indirectly (as in Galilee), was under the control of Rome, but he did not hint that Rome's control should be resisted. He appears to have followed in the tradition of Jeremiah and other prophets in viewing Gentile domination of Israel as divinely ordained for a particular time and purpose. As Jeremiah, six centuries before, had urged his people to seek the peace of the Babylonian Empire and warned them that their disobedience would result in the destruction of the temple at Jerusalem, so Jesus warned his contemporaries that, if the way of peace which he urged on them were not followed, the nation, city and temple alike would be involved in ruin.

He saw clearly that the way of the Zealots would lead to fearful disaster, and pleaded with the people to repent, to change their attitude and policy, before it was too late. It is in the highest degree improbable that this representation of Jesus' teaching should be a later and unhistorical construction. Had Jesus met his death at the hands of the occupying power for Zealot sympathies or activities, he would have won a place in Jewish memory alongside Judas Maccabaeus and others who fell in defence of national freedom. But that is not the kind of place that Jesus has in Jewish memory. Had he been minded to give a lead to the forces of armed resistance, the opportunity was available at the time of his feeding of the multitude in Galilee. He refused to grasp that opportunity when it was offered to him then, and that remained his policy to the end – a policy which, if his people had accepted it in preference to the Zealot policy, would have spared them the horrors which overtook them a generation later, culminating in the fall of the city and temple of Jerusalem in AD 70.

Essenes

Could Jesus then have been an Essene, or at least have had some association with the Essenes? The idea is one that has appealed to a number of students. It received widespread currency when the Irish writer George Moore worked it into the plot of his novel *The Brook Kerith*, first published in 1916. It must be said, however, that the idea is a suitable one for imaginative fiction, but has no place in historical fact.

But who were the Essenes? They were an order of pious Jews who lived the simple life in ascetic communities in the wilderness of Judaea and possibly in other areas within and on the borders of the holy land. They first appear in history around 150 BC. Those who were admitted to the order had to undergo a rigorous period of three years' probation. None of them retained any private property after final initiation; whatever they possessed passed at that time into the ownership of the community and was administered by its treasurer. They maintained themselves by undertaking various forms of manual labour. They devoted much time to the study of the sacred scriptures and interpreted the ancestral laws, especially the food laws and the laws of purity, with exceptional strictness.

Until 1947 our knowledge of the Essenes was derived almost entirely from ancient writers, whether pagans, like the Roman author Pliny the elder, Jews, like Philo of Alexandria and Josephus, or Christians, like Hippolytus of Rome. But when in 1947 the caves of the Qumran region, north-west of the Dead Sea, began to yield their manuscript treasures (the so-called Dead Sea Scrolls), it soon became clear that these documents had once belonged to the library of a religious community. It was natural to refer to this community as the Qumran community. And as more became known, from the study of the documents, about the life and beliefs of the community, many scholars concluded that it was a community of the Essene order. Indeed, when Pliny the elder, describing the Essenes as they existed before AD 70, says that they lived west of the Dead Sea, above Engedi, archaeologists who know the area assure us that there is only one site to which Pliny could have referred, that site being the headquarters of the Qumran community, thoroughly excavated from 1953 to 1956. If the Qumran community was indeed an Essene community (as is most probable), then the discoveries of 1947 and the following years have provided us with literature from inside the Essene order.[14]

The Qumran community was rigidly separatist. Its members believed that, by divine right, the office of high priest in Israel belonged exclusively to the house of Zadok. But there had been no high priest of the house of Zadok in Israel since 152 BC, when Jonathan, a brother of Judas Maccabaeus, received the sacred office. By the national constitution, the high priest was head of the theocratic state, and so those who denied his legitimacy could countenance no aspect of Jewish public life. The Pharisees, during most of the period with which we are concerned, were in opposition to the chief priesthood and its policies, but they played a full part in public life. The members of the Qumran community deplored the Pharisees' laxity in this regard, as well as in their interpretation and application of the laws of purity, and called them 'the seekers after smooth things' (or 'the givers of smooth interpretations'). To those who know the Pharisees only from the Gospels it may come as a surprise to learn that there were other Jews who criticised them for choosing the easy way in their observance of the law.

The Qumran community was organised, about 130 BC, by a leader whose name is not given; he is regularly called the Teacher of Righteousness (or perhaps the Rightful Guide). He was plainly an inspiring personality; he was also an original interpreter of the sacred scriptures. He taught his followers that they had a crucial part to play in the purpose of God for the winding up of the current age of wickedness and the inauguration of the new age of righteousness. As volunteers for holiness they might endure privation and persecution at the hand of ungodly authorities for the time being, but in due course they would be a chosen instrument in the hand of God for the execution of his righteous judgment on the wicked. If the New Testament presents John the Baptist as one sent to prepare the way for the coming of the Messiah, the Qumran literature ascribes much the same role to the Teacher of Righteousness.

We do not know how far other Essene groups shared the distinctive outlook of the Qumran community. There are said to have been around 4,000 Essenes in the middle of the first century AD; these may have included, in addition to members of the ascetic communities, sympathisers and well-wishers in the towns and villages of Israel. We are told that an Essene on a journey could always be sure of finding hospitality with a fellow-Essene; such fellow-Essenes who were in a position to provide hospitality might be called 'associate members' of the Essene order, leading ordinary lives here and there throughout the country. In the Gospel of Luke particularly we meet some people who were 'looking for the kingdom of God' or for 'the consolation of Israel'; such were Simeon of Jerusalem, who pronounced prophetic words when the infant Jesus was taken to the temple for the ceremony of purification, and Joseph of Arimathaea, who provided a tomb for Jesus' body.[15] It would be unwarranted to call such people Essenes, but they seem to have shared something of the Essenes' expectation. Again, when Jesus sent out his disciples two by two to announce the imminence of the kingdom of God, he told them, when they came to a town or village, to 'find out who is worthy in it' (Matthew 10:11) and stay with him till they left the place. It is not said expressly how the householder's 'worthiness' was to be ascertained, but he would presumably be in general sympathy with their mission. The situation would be at least analogous to that in which a travelling Essene found himself when he required a night's lodging.

But these considerations come nowhere near making Jesus an Essene. To be sure, when the Qumran manuscripts first came to light, and even more when the community's headquarters at Khirbet Qumran were excavated, there was some revival of the old fancy associating him with the Essenes. One

distinguished British archaeologist, giving an account in 1955
of the uncovering of the community's headquarters, was rash
enough to say, 'John the Baptist was almost certainly an
Essene, and must have studied and worked in this building; he
undoubtedly derived the idea of ritual immersion, or baptism,
from them. Many authorities consider that Christ Himself
also studied with them for some time. If that be so, then we
have in this little building something unique indeed, for alone
of all the ancient remains in Jordan,[16] this has remained
unchanged – indeed, unseen and unknown, to this day.
These, then, are the very walls He looked upon, the corridors
and rooms through which He wandered and in which He
sat.'[17]

These are no more than conjectures, although the conjecture that John the Baptist had some association with the
community is less improbable than the conjecture that Jesus
ever visited Khirbet Qumran. But when a leading archaeologist expressed himself in these terms, non-specialists might
reasonably suppose that there was some solid evidence in
support of his conjecture; and there was none. In the same
year an American literary critic, the late Edmund Wilson,
hazarded the suggestion that Khirbet Qumran 'is perhaps,
more than Bethlehem or Nazareth, the cradle of Christianity'.[18]

Others drew analogies between Jesus and the Qumran
Teacher of Righteousness, who preceded him by a century
and more. An eminent French Semitist, Professor A.
Dupont-Sommer, expressed his judgment that 'the Galilaean
Teacher, as he is presented to us in the New Testament
writings, appears in many respects as an astonishing re-
incarnation of the Teacher of Righteousness'.[19] A Jewish
scholar, J. L. Teicher, went further and concluded that the
Teacher of Righteousness was Jesus himself – the Qumran
community being, in his view, a sect of Jewish Christians
otherwise known as Ebionites. A corollary of Dr Teicher's
argument was that the great opponent and persecutor of the
Qumran community, referred to in the texts as the Wicked
Priest (actually one of the rulers of the Hasmonaean dynasty),

was Saul of Tarsus, Paul the apostle.[20] At the opposite extreme from this, an Australian scholar has, much more recently, suggested that the Wicked Priest was a term of disapproval applied to none other than Jesus by the followers of John the Baptist, the Teacher of Righteousness, after Jesus had launched out on his own.[21] But it is wise to understand the word 'priest' in the term the 'Wicked Priest' in its literal sense, and since neither Paul nor Jesus was a priest it renders this argument difficult to sustain.

The Qumran Teacher of Righteousness did not claim to be a Messiah, nor did his followers believe him to be one. After his death, they continued to look forward to the coming of the Messiah – some of them at least expected two Messiahs, a prince of the house of David and a priest of the house of Aaron.

How he died we do not know. Attacks were made on his life, but he appears to have survived them safely, and when his death is mentioned in the Qumran literature, it is called his 'gathering in' – that is, his being gathered in to join the rest of the blessed dead, an expression usually referring to natural death. There is no evidence that atoning significance was attached to his death. He did not rise from the dead, nor (so far as our evidence goes) did anyone ever believe he had done so.

In some details the teaching of Jesus exhibits resemblances to the teaching maintained in the Qumran community (which probably derived from the Teacher) but these are not pronounced enough to suggest strong affinities between the teachers. In his interpretation of the marriage law, for example, he appealed to the creation narrative which tells how in the beginning 'God made them male and female' (Genesis 1:27). So did the men of Qumran: they appealed to that text as an argument against polygamy, while Jesus appealed to it as an argument against divorce and remarriage. Jesus also appealed to the creation narrative in his interpretation of the sabbath law, but his interpretation of the sabbath law was poles removed from that favoured in the Qumran community. He was criticised for what was regarded as laxity in his

sabbath practice, but he took it for granted that his critics
would agree that an animal in distress should be relieved on
the sabbath, even if the relief involved some activity that
would strictly be classified as 'work'. But help on the sabbath
to an animal in distress is explicitly forbidden in the Qumran
legislation. It is not that the men of Qumran were intention-
ally callous, but they were convinced (misguidedly) that the
law of God took precedence over humanitarian considerations. In the eyes of the Pharisees the cultivation of holiness
involved a separatist way of life, and they found fault with
Jesus because he mingled so freely with people whose proximity (they were sure) could not help towards a closer walk with
God. But the men of Qumran, as we have seen, criticised the
Pharisees for their laxity in this regard: holiness, in their view,
could be assured only by a degree of separatism which
amounted to isolation (not to say insulation). Nothing could
be more unlike the way of Jesus. He did at times take his
followers into the wilderness for a period of rest, but his active
ministry was carried out in places where people were, not in
places where they were not, in the busy towns west of the
Galilaean lake, and at the end in the city of Jerusalem.
Nothing less like the Qumran ideal can be envisaged than his
procedure, and even if the Qumran community was a special
group within the general Essene order, the Qumran ideal was
one expression of the Essene way. Jesus was no Essene, and
his life and teaching cannot be understood in Essene terms.

Chapter
14

Jesus in Christian Experience

The present experience of Christ

The Jesus of history was a person whom his friends and associates could see, hear and touch. The Christ of faith is not accessible in those ways to sense-perception; he is known to faith (and that is why he is called the Christ of faith). But by faith he is known to be a person as real as the Jesus of history was known to be by sense. More than that: by faith he is known to be identical with the Jesus who was seen, heard and touched on earth.

The ancient creeds of the church, in the section which they devote to the person and work of Jesus Christ, the Son of God, affirm that, having become man, he 'was crucified also for us under Pontius Pilate. He suffered and was buried, and the third day he rose again according to the scriptures, and ascended into heaven, and sits at the Father's right hand. He shall come again with glory to judge both the living and the dead. His kingdom shall have no end.'

These affirmations are soundly based in the New Testament writings. The earlier ones relate to the Jesus of history, the later ones to the Christ of faith. But the only affirmation made with reference to the present time is that he 'sits at the Father's right hand'. This is pictorial language based, as we saw in discussing Jesus' interrogation by the high priest, on an oracle in one of the Old Testament psalms. Slightly less pictorial language is used in a primitive Christian hymn, quoted in Paul's letter to the church at Philippi,[1] which tells how, after Jesus' humiliation and crucifixion, 'God has highly exalted him and bestowed on him the name which is above every name', decreeing that every knee should bend at Jesus' name and every tongue confess that he is Lord.

But there is one highly important aspect of Jesus' present order of existence that the creeds pass over without mention. That is his abiding presence with his people. This is no mere matter of theory: it is something of which many Christians have been vitally aware in one generation after another since he was last seen on earth.

The evangelist Matthew reports Jesus' last words to the disciples before he was taken from them as a promise to be with them always, right on to the end (Matthew 28:20). The continuous fulfilment of that promise is amply documented in the New Testament – in Acts, the letters and the Revelation – and not only in the New Testament, but in the history of subsequent Christian experience.

One New Testament writer, claiming to be himself 'a witness of the sufferings of Christ', addresses fellow-Christians who had not shared that experience and says to them of Christ: 'Without having seen him you love him' (1 Peter 5:1; 1:8). Another, who had personally seen, heard and touched the one in whom (he declares) the eternal life of God was manifested, writes to believers of a younger generation to share with them what he himself had seen and heard, so that they in their turn may have fellowship 'with the Father and with his Son Jesus Christ' and reflect the love of him who first loved them (1 John 1:1–4; 4:19).

The witness of Paul

But in the New Testament writings the most intense and immediate consciousness of the personal knowledge and love of the Christ of faith is expressed by a man who in all probability never met and certainly never followed the Jesus of history. This man was Paul of Tarsus. In his younger days Paul set himself to oppose all that Jesus of Nazareth stood for,

and regarded him with abhorrence as one who died the death
on which the curse of God was explicitly pronounced. Yet,
less than twenty years after the death of Jesus, the total
reassessment of his person and work which was part of Paul's
Damascus-road experience moved him to view that death as
having been endured on his behalf: he speaks of Jesus as 'the
Son of God, who loved me and gave himself for me' (Galatians 2:20). These words have been repeatedly quoted and are
familiar to many Christians (who indeed are encouraged to
take them over and apply them to themselves). But it is only
familiarity with them that can blind us to their amazing
significance. What was there in the historical event of the
death of Jesus, and what was there in the gospel which Paul
'received', that could make him see that death as a voluntary
sacrifice specifically offered on his personal account? True,
the Son of Man was to give his life as a ransom for many; but
even if Paul knew that saying, what could have led him to
suppose that he, with his record as a persecutor of the
followers of Jesus, was included among those 'many'?

The answer to these questions, as to so many other questions relating to Paul's Christian experience and his presentation of the gospel, must lie in his call and commissioning on
the Damascus road. When we have put together all the
information given to us about that experience, whether by
Paul himself in his letters or by Luke in Acts, there are many
features in it which escape us. But the total experience, in
Paul's own words, was 'a revelation of Jesus Christ'; that is to
say, it was the occasion when God, as he goes on to say,
revealed his Son not only *to* Paul but *in* him (Galatians
1:12,16). This revelation, in which the risen Christ was seen
by Paul and spoke to him personally, marked the beginning of
Paul's personal acquaintance with Christ. He knew him as
intimately as anyone can know a close friend. There was no
doubt of the identity of this risen Christ with the crucified
Jesus: this is plain both from Paul's letters and from the record
of Acts, where the risen Christ introduces himself to Paul with
the words: 'I am Jesus of Nazareth' (Acts 22:8).

Any attempt to estimate the validity of Paul's Damascus-

road experience must reckon with the dynamic which it
provided for his activity and achievement as Christ's apostle
to the Gentiles during the following thirty years, and with the
lasting effects of his apostleship. It was not without reason
that an eighteenth-century writer, George Lyttelton,
observed that 'the conversion and apostleship of St Paul
alone, duly considered, was of itself a demonstration sufficient to prove Christianity to be a divine revelation'.[2]

The beginning of Paul's personal acquaintance with Christ
carried with it the beginning of his exceptional insight into the
mind of Christ. This unsurpassed insight is abundantly
attested by a detailed comparison of Paul's ministry with his
Lord's works and words. It is not only that Paul's central
teaching about the sovereignty of God's grace, and the call to
men and women to respond to that grace in faith, is based
on the teaching of the historical Jesus – teaching which we
know from the Gospels, but which Paul knew from those
who heard it. It is that Paul shows remarkable sureness of
touch in drawing out features which were only implicit in the
ministry of the historical Jesus and in giving them practical
effect.

That Paul was the personal object of the Son of God's
self-sacrificing love was part of what he learned on the
Damascus road. Not that he was the only beneficiary of that
love: he might have said, like a trophy of divine grace in later
days:

> I knew that Christ had given me birth
> To brother all the souls on earth.[3]

In fact, it would be difficult to name any aspect of Paul's
gospel or of his Christian thought which was not present,
implicitly at least, in the Damascus-road 'revelation of Jesus
Christ'.

When Paul puts that experience 'last of all' in a sequence of
resurrection appearances of Christ to Peter, James and others
who were followers of Jesus well before Paul himself, he may
suggest that what happened on the Damascus road belonged

in a different category from his later experiences of the
presence of Christ.

These later experiences, nevertheless, played an important
part in Paul's Christian life. When he repeats the language of
early Christian confession, he speaks of 'Christ Jesus who
died, yes, who was raised from the dead, who is at the right
hand of God, who indeed intercedes for us' (Romans 8:34).
But when he expresses himself more personally, he does not
confine the present work of Christ to his making intercession
for his people in the presence of God; he speaks of him as one
whom he knows to be constantly present with him, one with
whom he can communicate directly. At certain critical junc-
tures, too, he was assured of his Lord's nearness and encouragement in a particularly vivid way. He is normally
reticent about such 'visions and revelations of the Lord' (2
Corinthians 12:1). Others, with much less justification, might
boast about such experiences, but those which came Paul's
way were too sacred for such unworthy treatment, and sometimes too poignant, like the strange ecstasy of which he tells
his Corinthian friends, when he was 'caught up into Paradise
. . . and heard things that cannot be told' (2 Corinthians
12:3,4). In fact, he has more to say about the aftermath of that
experience than about the experience itself; but the aftermath
involved a person-to-person encounter between Paul and his
Lord, in which he begged repeatedly for the removal of the
recurring 'thorn in the flesh' – the agony which he had to
endure as the sequel to the ecstasy. The response to his plea
was not the removal of his humiliating and embarrassing
affliction, but the assurance of sufficient grace from Christ to
help him not only to endure it but actually to glory in it.

In Acts we find mention made of three occasions on which
the Lord appeared and spoke to him in the course of his
apostolic activities: in the temple during his first visit to
Jerusalem after his conversion (Acts 22:17–21); early in his
ministry at Corinth, when he received encouragement to
counteract the apprehension with which he began his work
there (Acts 18:9,10); and later, in a time of great danger
during his last visit to Jerusalem (Acts 23:11). On these

occasions Paul received direction and reassurance of which he found himself in conscious need. To these may be added a further occasion when he made a court appearance (probably in Rome) and all those on whose support he might have relied deserted him – but, as he says, 'the Lord stood by me and gave me strength to proclaim the message fully, that all the Gentiles might hear it' (2 Timothy 4:16,17).

These experiences, whether related by Luke or described by Paul himself, provide evidence, in some people's eyes, for regarding Paul as a mystic. Much depends on the definition of the term 'mystic'; much depends also on one's estimate of the validity of mystical experience. But Paul usually refers to such experiences in the most matter-of-fact way (he admits to uncertainty about the nature of the ecstatic experience mentioned in 2 Corinthians 12:2–4). He does not imply that such experiences were peculiar to himself or to a privileged minority. On the contrary: the awareness of the presence of Christ, as a living reality, should be enjoyed by all his people. When Paul tells the Philippian Christians to have no anxiety because 'The Lord is at hand' (Philippians 4:5), he is not referring (not primarily, at any rate) to the approach of the Second Advent but to the risen Lord's personal nearness to his people. Their realisation of his nearness should fill their hearts with peace and joy, even (or indeed especially) in the most trying circumstances of life. The Jesus of history, if he were that and nothing more, might seem remote and inaccessible, but as the Christ of faith he is close at hand and accessible.

It is a common experience to have a strange sense of the presence of one whom we have known but who is no longer with us. This is something which, together with their memory and influence, may live on after they themselves have died and may continue to exercise a profound and practical effect. Or one may study the life and work of a person of the more remote past – especially if he is given to wearing his heart on his sleeve, as Paul (for example) so often does in his writings – to the point where it is possible to develop a rare personal appreciation of him, or even empathy with him. But the living presence of the Christ of faith is not analogous to experiences like these. The example of Paul is especially important in this regard. It was not the memory of the historical Jesus (although their lives overlapped), nor was it a study of his earthly ministry, that accounted for the place which Christ came to have in Paul's life. It was as the risen Lord that Paul first came to know him, and that personal knowledge increased with the passing of time. However well Paul came to know the Lord, there was always more of him to know. To the end of his days his chief ambition was still to 'gain Christ', to know Christ, to enter more fully into the experiences of Christ, in his death and resurrection, so that, as far as possible, those experiences might become Paul's too.

When human beings live together in an interpersonal relationship or as members of a closely knit community, there tends to be a certain merging of their personalities. That might suggest an analogy for Paul's experience of the Christ of faith, except that here the merging was not reciprocal; it was the merging of Paul's life in Christ's (without any impairment of Paul's personality in the process). Thus Paul can say, 'it is no longer I who live, but Christ who lives in me; and the life I now live in the flesh I live by faith in the Son of God' (Galatians 2:20).

The reader may think that this account of Paul's Christian experience is a digression. But that is not really so. Our subject is Jesus Christ, the Jesus of history who is also the Christ of faith, and in Paul's experience of Christ it is Christ who is active; Christ is the true subject. Paul at any rate insisted that this was so: 'it is no longer I who live, but Christ who lives in me'. Mention has already been made of Paul's activity and achievement as Christ's apostle to the Gentiles. But when Paul thought about his activity and achievement, he preferred to speak of 'what Christ has accomplished through me' (Romans 15:18). The Christ who lived in him was the one who worked through him.

The continually active Christ

Among the New Testament writers, Paul is not alone in this perspective. When Luke, at the beginning of the second volume of his history of Christian beginnings, says that the former volume was concerned with 'all that Jesus began to do and teach, until the day when he was taken up' (Acts 1:1,2), the implication is that the new volume will deal with what Jesus *continued* to do and teach from then on. That is to say, the Christ who died and rose again remains alive and active *on earth* – though no longer visibly present – by his Spirit in his followers. This is what Luke's second volume is about. And the story which the Acts of the Apostles begins to tell is a story which has not yet come to an end: the living Christ is still at work on earth through his people, as they are empowered by his Spirit.

This is not the place to deal in detail with the Holy Spirit in the sense in which he has been abroad in the world since the death and resurrection of Jesus.[4] However, it is significant that the Holy Spirit is expressly called 'the Spirit of Jesus' or 'the Spirit of Christ', because it is not only by the Spirit's power that the risen Christ works on through his followers but he is also the one who makes the abiding presence of Christ so real and vivid to them.

The way in which the Christ of faith can be personally known to those who never knew him as the Jesus of history has been illustrated especially from Paul's experience because he was a Christian of the first generation who has placed his knowledge of Christ on record in his writings. But other Christians than Paul, while they have not shared his Damascus-road revelation, have shared his personal knowledge of the indwelling Christ. Even if they have not experienced it with the same intensity, or expressed their experience with the same assurance, they have at least found in the experience to which he gave such memorable expression an ideal which they have earnestly sought to realise. Its realisation would be a vain hope apart from the living power of the Christ of faith; but it is not dependent on the effort of their own will or imagination. He who 'was crucified in weakness' is the one who now 'lives by the power of God' (2 Corinthians 13:3,4), and he therefore remains powerful in his people's lives.

Chapter
15

The Son of God

The Son and the children

To the question 'Who is Jesus?' the Nicene Creed answers that he is 'the only-begotten Son of God, begotten of his Father before all worlds . . .' The Nicene Creed, like other ancient formulae in which Christians have traditionally confessed their faith, is couched in an idiom of its own, which is different from that of the New Testament.[1] Its affirmations, though distinctive, are based on the witness of the New Testament; they have no independent validity apart from that witness. And the witness of the New Testament is essentially the witness of Jesus – first the witness borne by him and then the witness borne to him. Councils and creeds, according to a statement already quoted in these pages, 'must wholly rest upon the history of our Lord Jesus Christ.'[2]

We have seen how the Roman centurion in charge of the squad of soldiers who carried out the work of crucifixion on the day when Jesus and two others were executed outside the wall of Jerusalem, was strangely impressed by the manner of Jesus' death. 'In truth', he exclaimed, 'this man was the Son of God!' (Mark 15:39).[3] What this non-commissioned officer meant by those words must be a matter of speculation; certainly he meant nothing like what the Nicene Creed means. Men of exceptional nobility of character and bearing were sometimes called 'divine men' in those days; perhaps he meant something like that. His meaning would better be expressed by the rendering 'this man was *a* son of God'. But

Mark the evangelist, in reporting this incident, seizes on the centurion's words as summing up the theme of his Gospel, and gives them the full significance: 'this man was *the* Son of God'.

The opening sentence of Mark's Gospel, according to the common text, sets forth the subject-matter of the work: 'The beginning of the gospel of Jesus Christ, the Son of God' (Mark 1:1). There is, however, some doubt whether or not the phrase 'the Son of God' was part of the original wording here (although more probably it was). But there is no doubt about the wording of the heavenly voice which greeted Jesus at his baptism, and which Mark reports a few sentences further down. 'You are my Son, my beloved one', said the voice; 'with you I am well pleased' (Mark 1:11). The evangelist reports this as a personal assurance addressed to Jesus. Midway through his Gospel, he reports a similar utterance from heaven, this time addressed to the disciples who were with Jesus at the time of his transfiguration: 'This is my Son, my beloved one; listen to him!' (Mark 9:7). From his baptism to his crucifixion, then, Jesus is presented by Mark as the Son of God.

Not only Mark, but practically all the New Testament writers, acknowledge Jesus as the Son of God. They associate this relationship with various points in his career – his conception, his birth, his baptism, his recognition at Caesarea Philippi, his transfiguration, his trial, his death, his resurrection, his exaltation. But none of them implies that he became the Son of God for the first time at any of those points. Paul, for example, says that he was 'designated Son of God in power according to the Spirit of holiness by his resurrection from the dead' (Romans 1:4); but Paul does not mean that Jesus first became Son of God when he was raised from death. Paul knows, and says, that Jesus was already God's Son when he was sent into the world; he means that by his resurrection the one who had been the Son of God on earth in humility and obscurity was now effectively proclaimed to be Son of God to all who had ears to hear.

But what exactly is meant by Jesus' being the Son of God?

We know what 'son' means in the literal, biological sense; but that sense is not in view when Jesus is called the Son of God. When the Qur'ān denies categorically that God ever had a son (from which denial it would follow that Jesus was not the Son of God), it is the biological relation that is intended.[4] Either Muhammad misunderstood Christians when they confessed that Jesus was the Son of God, or the Christians with whom he was in touch misunderstood their own confession.

Actually, part of what the New Testament means by calling Jesus the Son of God is conveyed in the Qur'ān when it speaks of him as God's 'Word'.[5] In the Gospel of John especially – the Gospel which begins with the statement 'In the beginning was the Word' – the Son of God is pre-eminently the revealer of the Father.[6] 'Son', to that extent, is the equivalent of 'Word'. John's statement that 'the Word became flesh and dwelt among us' (John 1:14) is another way of saying that 'God sent his only Son into the world, so that we might live through him' (1 John 4:9). Whether he is called the Son or the Word, Jesus is the self-expression of God. 'Whoever has seen me', he says to Philip, 'has seen the Father' (John 14:9). 'No one knows the Father except the Son', he says elsewhere, 'and any one to whom the Son chooses to reveal him' (Matthew 11:27; see Luke 10:22). The words he spoke, the works he performed, the life he led, the person he was – all disclosed the unseen Father. He is, in Paul's words, the visible 'image of the invisible God' (Colossians 1:15).

But more than this is involved in Jesus' being the Son of God. The inmost meaning of the title is bound up with his intense and constant awareness of God as his Father. While this awareness finds its clearest expression in the Gospel of John, John simply makes explicit what is present in the whole gospel record. Jesus enjoyed an unbroken sense of the presence and fellowship of God as his Father. So intimate was this fellowship that he used the family word 'Abba' when speaking to God or speaking about him, and he taught his disciples to do the same. He knew himself to be commissioned by his Father to fulfil a special work on earth, and the consciousness of doing his Father's will was his dearest delight. He is most properly called the Son of God because he knew himself to stand in that relation to his heavenly Father.

To ask if Jesus knew himself to be the Second Person of the Trinity is to try to formulate his inner consciousness in the vocabulary of a later age,[7] which for the Jesus of history would have had no meaning. We may choose to express our understanding of his person in such language, but for Jesus himself it is sufficient to say that he knew himself to be the Father's dear Son, responding to the Father's love with a full response of obedient love. It was his prime mission in life to communicate the Father's love to others, not only in his teaching but also in his action and suffering, and to bring them into that enjoyment of it which was so real to himself.

Jesus, then, was eager that his followers should enter into that relationship of filial love to God which was antecedently and distinctively his. This thought is expressed by John when he says that it is to all who have received him that Christ has given the right, the authority, to become children of God – 'to all', that is, 'who believe in his name' (John 1:12). Through their believing in Christ they are united with him, and enter by a new and heavenly birth into the family of God, in which Christ (to use Paul's language) is 'the first-born among many brothers' (Romans 8:29). Those who belong to this family bear the family likeness. That is to say, they reproduce the character of Christ, who displays the character of the Father. Jesus implied this when he told his disciples to show by their lives that they were children of God, merciful to others as he is merciful to all.[8]

Considerations like these put flesh and blood on the language of the historic creeds, when they speak of Christ (for example) as being 'of one substance with the Father'.[9] This form of words, devised in the fourth century in the course of controversies which were rife at that time, means that it is the one living and true God whom Jesus reveals because he shares the essence and nature of that one living and true God. Jesus is not to be thought of as a secondary deity alongside the supreme God. As the Son, he is the very expression of the Father; in him we see 'the human face of God'.[10]

Jesus the intercessor

It is important to emphasise this continuity of expression and character, because language has sometimes been used which could suggest that Jesus is more merciful than God, that he is strenuously engaged in persuading God to be merciful. Jesus did not die to make God love the human race; he died to display God's love for the human race and his resolve to save it from disaster and destruction. To talk as if he died so as to make God relent and bestow forgiveness where previously he had been bent on vengeance is to perpetrate a travesty both of Christ's atoning work and of the Father's character. When Jesus is said to be interceding now with God on his people's behalf, it is not as though God were reluctant to show his grace and had to be won over by earnest and tearful entreaties. This intercessor is the one whom God delights to honour, whom he has already exalted to 'the highest place that heaven affords', to whom he can deny nothing that he asks for.

But what is the nature of Jesus' present 'intercession' with the Father? It may be described as his procuring and making available for his people all the help they need to live the Christian life, whether in crises or in the normal course of existence. This was a service which he performed for his friends when he was with them on earth. There was, for example, an occasion when Peter was to face a crisis of faith which might well have put an end to all hope of his ever doing anything useful in the cause of Christ. This was the crisis in which Peter, for all his boast of unswerving loyalty, denied all knowledge of Jesus. 'Satan', Jesus told him, 'wants to put you and your companions through the mill' (our colloquial equivalent for 'sift you like wheat'). 'But', he went on, 'I have been praying for you, that your faith may not collapse; and when you have been restored, strengthen the others' (Luke 22:31,32). Jesus prayed, that is to say, that God would give Peter strength to confess his Lord or, if he failed in that, strength to recover his own faith and loyalty and to help his companions to recover theirs. What he did then for Peter he continues to do for his people, not only by praying for them but by his very presence with God as the one who by his death has atoned for their sins and won for them that direct access to God which is his by right. Children are not restricted by protocol in approaching their father: 'in Christ Jesus', says Paul, 'you are all sons of God through faith' (Galatians 3:26).

The inclusive Christ

This phrase, 'in Christ Jesus' (or 'in Christ'), calls for more than cursory attention. The witness of several New Testament writers is that Jesus, now exalted as Lord of the universe, does not merely save and help his people by remote control; he is present with them and, indeed, lives within them. Nor is this witness confined to New Testament writers; it has been the witness of Christians in every succeeding generation, as they have tried to put into words their experience of Christ as a present and vital reality. 'Christ lives in me' was the way in which Paul summed it up (Galatians 2:20), and in doing so he spoke for many others. The power of Christ's resurrection life is imparted to his people, who are united to him by faith.

But if Christ lives in his people, the statement can be put the other way round: they live in him. The Christian life is not a solitary business; it must be lived out in community with others. Those in whom the risen Christ lives through faith share that imparted life with one another. According to the New Testament, that life is communicated to them and maintained within them by the Spirit of Christ. Paul has his own distinctive way of expressing this experience: Christians, according to him, are incorporated in Christ, they are members of his body. Being members of the body of Christ in this sense, individual believers are viewed as limbs or organs, each discharging its appropriate functions under the control of the head for the health and efficiency of the whole body. In the most fully developed form of this body-figure (presented in the letters to the Colossians and to the Ephesians) Christ himself is the head. Christ is portrayed both as the individual

Christ, to whom his people are united by faith, and as the corporate Christ – Christ himself plus his people.

This teaching about union with Christ or incorporation in him might lend itself to mysticism. But only a minority are called to be mystics; this teaching is intended not for a minority but for all Christians, and it is given a very practical thrust. Members of Christ are his instruments, or agents, for doing his work in the world.

Another New Testament writer who expresses similar ideas is John. He has much to say about the people of Christ 'abiding' or 'dwelling' in him and of his 'abiding' in them. Because of the mutual love of God and Christ – the Father and the Son – to 'abide' in Christ is to 'abide' in God and to have Christ 'abiding' in his people is to have God 'abiding' in them. But this mutual indwelling, although it appears to be a mystical conception, is very practical; it is bound up with the way people live. 'Anyone who claims to dwell in him should lead the same kind of life as he led' (1 John 2:6). 'If we love one another, God dwells in us . . . any one who dwells in love dwells in God, and God dwells in him' (1 John 4:12,16).

Unlike Paul, John does not use the figure of the body of Christ; instead, his teaching about the mutual indwelling of Christ and his people is expressed in the parable of the true vine, spoken by Jesus to his disciples in the upper room on the night in which he was betrayed (John 15:1–11). 'I am the vine, you are the branches', he said to them (verse 5). The branches can produce grapes only if they 'abide' in the vine, remain in vital contact with the parent stem and draw their sustenance and fertility from it. Similarly, it is only by remaining in union with Christ that his people can lead 'fruitful' lives – fruitful not only in the development of the Christian graces but also in the influence for good which they exercise on the lives of others, showing to them the love which they themselves have been shown by Christ. As love is the foremost 'fruit of the Spirit' for Paul, so for John love is the principal Christian grace – one indeed which comprises all the others and enables those in whom it is found to share in the fellowship of love that eternally unites the Father and the Son.

The idea of mutual indwelling or of incorporation into Christ may be difficult to grasp in relation to common experience. Yet there are many Christians whose way of life is directed not only by the example and teaching of the historical Jesus but also by an inner power greater than their own – the power of the ever-living Christ communicated to them and made effective in them by his Spirit. The lives of such people are extensions of the life of Christ. We can all appreciate how a person like Mother Theresa may be described in this way; she is a member of Christ whom he uses to carry on his ministry of loving care among those who need it most. But it is the function of all the followers of Christ to be the instruments of his grace in the world, and they can be so if they remain in living touch with him. If we ask 'Who is Jesus?' in the present tense, part of the answer must lie in his present life and activity as the corporate Christ.

This corporate Christ with whom his people are united and whose risen life and power flow through them to others is the Son of God, the revealer of the Father. It is for this reason that his people become, in the daring words of one New Testament writer, 'partakers of the divine nature' (2 Peter 1:4). It is in this partaking that true immortality consists. For Jesus, one with God yet becoming one of us, has bridged the gap between God and humanity, between Creator and creation. 'The Son of God became the Son of Man so that the children of men might become the children of God.'[11] But Paul compresses all this, and more, into seven words addressed to a community of Christians whom he had never met: 'Christ in you, the hope of glory' (Colossians 1:27).

Chapter
16

The Incarnate Word

'In the beginning was the Word'

We have seen how an early Christian hymn celebrates Jesus as the one who, because of his willing submission to humiliation and death, has been elevated by God to a position of supremacy over the universe and invested with the title 'Lord' – 'the name high over all'.[1] But that hymn opens with a statement that goes back before the time when Jesus' human life began. 'He always existed in the form of God', it says, 'but did not regard his equality with God as something to be exploited for his own advantage. Instead of that, he divested himself of all that he had and took the form of a servant' (Philippians 2:6–11). These words do not mean that he *exchanged* 'the form of God' *for* 'the form of a servant', but rather that he *manifested* the form of God *in* the form of a servant. When, at the last supper, he took a servant's place and washed his disciples' feet, he was revealing the nature of the God as much as in any of his other actions. The word 'form' does not imply that he was an actor playing a variety of parts, now the part of God and now the part of a servant; it implies that he shared the true nature of God and displayed that nature on earth by serving others. To serve others was something that came naturally to him.

What concerns us at present, however, is this: the hymn seems to assume that he existed already before he entered human life. The same assumption is shared by a number of New Testament writers; but it is asserted in the most forthright terms by John the evangelist at the outset of the fourth Gospel. 'In the beginning was the Word', he says, 'and the Word was with God, and the Word was God . . . And the Word became flesh and took up residence among us' (John 1:1,14). It is this statement, that 'the Word became flesh', that is expanded in the doctrine of the incarnation.

Since 'the Word' became flesh as the man Jesus of Nazareth, 'the Word' is a title of the Jesus of history. On becoming 'flesh', the eternal Word of God entered history. But the title also belongs to Jesus as the Christ of faith; it was the insight of faith that bestowed it on him, not during his earthly career but after his death and resurrection.

What, then, is this Word that was with God in the beginning, sharing the being and nature of God – this Word that in due course 'became flesh'? It is the self-revelation or self-expression of God. God, who revealed or expressed himself in many ways before the coming of Christ (as he still does), has given us the supreme and perfect revelation or expression of his nature in this man Jesus.

The Gospel of John opens designedly with the same phrase as the book of Genesis: 'In the beginning'. 'In the beginning' when, according to Genesis, God created the universe, the Word, says John, was with him. More than that, the Word was his agent in the work of creation: 'all things came into being through him' (John 1:3). It was this identical Word, moreover, that 'became flesh' in Jesus of Nazareth.

This is the origin of the traditional Christian language which ascribes the work of creation to Jesus. The second stanza of the hymn 'All hail the power of Jesus' name' – omitted from many modern collections – puts it thus:

> Crown him, ye morning stars of light,
> Who launched this floating ball;
> Now hail the Strength of Israel's might
> And crown him Lord of all.

'This floating ball' is the earth, and Jesus is said to have 'launched' it (or, according to *Hymns Ancient and Modern*,

to have 'fixed' it). Those who are familiar with this kind
of language probably do not often stop to reflect how astounding it is. A man who lived in the Near East just
under two thousand years ago is credited with creating the
world aeons before that. How could such an idea have
occurred to the minds of even the most devoted of his
followers?

The creation narrative of Genesis 1 records that 'God said',
and that in consequence successive phases of his creative
work came into being. 'God said, "Let there be light"'; and
there was light . . . God said, "Let us make man . . .", so God
created man' (Genesis 1:3,26,27). More poetical parts of the
Old Testament speak of this work as carried out by the word
of God. 'By the word of the Lord the heavens were made'
(Psalm 33:6) is another way of saying 'he spoke, and it came to
be' (Psalm 33:9). The word of God is thus personified as his
agent in creation. Elsewhere in the Old Testament the same
word is personified as God's agent in revelation (as when 'the
word of the Lord came' to this prophet and that) and in
salvation: when people in fear for their life cried to God for
help, 'he sent forth his word, and healed them, and delivered
them from destruction' (Psalm 107:20).

God's word is thus personified as his agent or messenger.
But language which is used as a figure of speech in the Old
Testament is used by John in the prologue to his Gospel to
express not merely personification but real and distinctive
personality. As the historical Jesus was truly personal, so
(according to John) the divine Word that 'became flesh' in
him was truly personal from the beginning, enjoying interpersonal fellowship with God and participating in his nature.
This is an aspect of the Christ of faith at which we have not
previously looked in our present study. We have considered
the risen and exalted Christ as the present object of his
people's faith; but the Gospel of John sets him forth as the
eternally pre-existent one who spent a few years on earth,
passing through the genuine human experiences of birth and
death, on his way from glory back to glory. John indeed is not
the only New Testament writer to use the language of pre-

existence with reference to him, but he uses it more explicitly than any of the others.

It is only in the prologue that the Gospel of John speaks of Jesus as the Word. It is as though the prologue were intended to serve notice to the readers of the Gospel that, in everything which the Gospel goes on to record of the works and words of Jesus, this is the Word of God in action; this is God expressing himself.

Where the prologue speaks of 'the Word' and 'God', the body of the Gospel speaks of 'the Son' and 'the Father'. The prologue covers the first eighteen verses of the Gospel, and right at the end it states that the only-begotten one, 'who has his being in the Father's bosom' (that is, who enjoys a perfect and loving mutual understanding with the Father), is the one who has 'declared' him. This statement of John 1:18 forms the transition from the prologue to the body of the Gospel. In the Gospel of John the Son is the mirror-image of the Father, so that anyone who has seen the Son has seen the Father. The Son and the Father exist together in an eternal relationship of reciprocal love, and all those who are united to the Son through believing in him are welcomed into this relationship: the Father of Jesus becomes their Father too.

But already in the earlier Gospels Jesus displays an intense filial awareness as he speaks of God as his Father. He is 'the Son' in a unique sense; nevertheless he encourages his disciples to call God their Father ('Abba') and to approach him with the same implicit confidence as he himself enjoys. The Gospel of John simply spells this out in fuller detail. The synoptic Gospels represent the disciples and others as wondering from time to time who Jesus really is: 'Who then is this, that even wind and sea obey him?' (Mark 4:41). But John lets his readers into the secret from the first words of his Gospel, while he makes it plain that the disciples did not grasp the secret until after their master's resurrection.

The creative Wisdom

Apart from the Gospel of John, the only New Testament document to call Jesus the Word of God expressly is the book of the Revelation, which comes from the same circle, if not from the same individual author. John the seer describes a vision of the warrior-Messiah in which an inscription proclaims him to be 'The Word of God' (Revelation 19:13). But if other New Testament writers do not use the title 'Word' in this personal sense, some of them do use or allude to another designation of Jesus which makes much the same point.

This designation is 'the wisdom of God'. For example, Paul reminds his converts in Corinth that the gospel of Christ crucified is, by secular standards, sheer foolishness; nevertheless, the fact that this gospel accomplishes a saving work in the lives of those who accept it, such as the loftiest Greek philosophy could not accomplish, confirms the claim that Christ crucified is 'the power of God and the wisdom of God' (1 Corinthians 1:24). He is the one, Paul repeats, 'whom God made our wisdom' (1 Corinthians 1:30).

In the Old Testament, especially in those documents which make up the 'wisdom' literature (notably Job, Proverbs, and a few of the psalms), the wisdom of God is credited with the creative agency which is elsewhere ascribed to the word of God. If, as we have seen, Psalm 33:6 says that 'by the *word* of the Lord the heavens were made', Proverbs 3:19 says that 'The Lord by *wisdom* founded the earth; by understanding he established the heavens'. In this statement 'wisdom' is simply an abstract noun, parallel to 'understanding'; it is an attribute of God. But there are other places in the wisdom literature where 'wisdom' is personified. The most notable of these places is Proverbs 8:22–31. There Wisdom speaks in the first person singular as the eldest and best-loved child of the Almighty, his companion before the world was made, serving him as a master-workman when creation's work began.

John the evangelist launches his Gospel with the threefold declaration that the Word existed in the beginning, that the Word was with God, and that the Word was God. Then he repeats part of that declaration in the next sentence by saying that 'He was in the beginning with God' (John 1:2). But when he does that, he is not indulging in mere repetition for the sake of repetition. He is concerned rather to say, 'This "Word" that I have just spoken about is identical with the "Wisdom" which, according to the book of Proverbs, was at God's side as "the beginning of his way".'

When Wisdom speaks in the first person in the book of Proverbs, this is an instance of personification, a figure of speech. But when John speaks of the Word at the beginning of his Gospel, he is using no mere figure of speech; he ascribes real personality to the Word. This is recognised in those English translations which refer to the Word in the prologue of this Gospel not as 'it', but as 'he' or 'him'. 'All things came into being through *him*, and apart from *him* nothing that exists came into being' (John 1:3). The implication is that the Word existed as a distinct person, the willing agent of God, before becoming 'flesh' and making his home with men and women.

So, when Christ was called the wisdom of God, the wisdom of God was identified as a real person. If the Old Testament spoke of the world as created by the divine wisdom, then it followed that Christ, before his appearance on earth, was the one 'through whom all things . . . exist' (1 Corinthians 8:6) or, more fully, the one in whom, through whom and for whom 'all things were created' (Colossians 1:16). The statement that '*in* him all things were created' suggests that he is 'the beginning' *in* which, according to Genesis 1:1, God created heaven and earth. This identification of Christ with 'the beginning' was facilitated by the language of Proverbs 8:22 where Wisdom claims to be 'the beginning' of God's way. A remarkable parallel to this appears in Revelation 3:14 where the letter to the church of Laodicea (one of the seven churches of Asia) is headed: 'The words of the Amen, the faithful and true witness, the beginning of God's creation.' Like the other letters to the seven churches, this letter is sent through John the seer by the risen Christ, who designates himself by various titles in the introduction to the successive letters. In this letter he identifies himself, by implication, with the divine Wisdom; in the phrase 'the beginning of God's creation' the reference to Genesis 1:1 ('In the beginning God created the heavens and the earth') and Proverbs 8:22 ('The Lord possessed me as the beginning of his way') cannot be mistaken. (The title 'the Amen' means something like 'steadfast and sure'; an attempt has been made to link it with the 'master workman' of Proverbs 8:30, the Hebrew word for which is *'āmôn*, but this is unconvincing.)

The same wisdom background is presupposed in the opening words of the letter to the Hebrews, where the Son of God is said to be the one 'through whom also he created the world' (Hebrews 1:2). The unknown writer of this letter goes on to describe the Son of God as 'upholding the universe by his word of power' (Hebrews 1:3); this is paralleled in Colossians 1:17, where it is said that 'in him all things hold together'.

Here, then, the same theme – Jesus as the creative Wisdom of God – finds expression in the work of three separate New Testament writers: Paul of Tarsus, John of Patmos, and the author of the letter to the Hebrews. It is probable that all three derived it from one source, and this source must have been a primitive one. The theme appears in Paul's writings not more than twenty-five years after the death and resurrection of Jesus; but Paul was not its originator. Moreover, the book of Revelation is not in the slightest degree indebted to Paul; it represents an independent strand in early Christianity.

Could the primitive source on which all three writers drew be found in the language of Jesus himself? Perhaps it could. When his teaching is classified according to the various forms in which it was presented or handed down, one of these forms is frequently categorised as 'wisdom sayings' – that is to say, utterances in which the speaker adopts the role of Wisdom, following a pattern familiar from the book of Proverbs and other Israelite wisdom literature. An outstanding example appears in Matthew 11:28–30: 'Come to me . . . Take my yoke upon you, and learn from me' – one of the 'comfortable words' of 'our Saviour Christ' by which the communicant is encouraged to approach his table in the Prayer Book order of Holy Communion. This invitation may be compared with an earlier invitation to enrol as pupils in the school of Wisdom: 'Draw near to me . . . Put your necks under the yoke, and let your souls receive instruction' (Sirach 51:23–26). It is not that Jesus, or the evangelist who records this utterance, quoted explicitly from the wisdom book of the son of Sirach (sometimes called Ecclesiasticus); but the form of the utterance was characteristic of 'wisdom sayings'. In the invitation reported by Matthew in his Gospel, it is divine Wisdom that speaks, but divine Wisdom embodied in 'our Saviour Christ'.

The image of God

It has been mentioned above that in the Gospel of John the Son is the mirror-image of the Father. But this is true not only of the Gospel of John. The writer to the Hebrews uses language to the same effect when he describes the Son as the effulgence of the Father's glory, bearing 'the very stamp of his nature' (Hebrews 1:3). In this language, again, we can discern an echo of wisdom literature. For example, in the Alexandrian book of Wisdom, written not many decades before the New Testament documents, wisdom is said to be 'a breath of the power of God, and a pure emanation of the glory of the Almighty . . . a reflection of eternal light, a spotless mirror of the working of God, and an image of his goodness' (Wisdom 7:25,26). Here is a further instance of the way in which a figure of speech in earlier wisdom literature becomes personal in the New Testament when it is applied to Christ, the Wisdom of God.

But among the New Testament writers it is Paul who most distinctively and explicitly speaks of Christ as the image of God. When Paul speaks in this way, we recognise in his words no mere literary echo but the impression made on him by the revelation of the glorified Christ which he received on the Damascus road. He says, for example, in one of his letters to the Christians of Corinth that 'the god of this world has blinded the minds of the unbelievers, to keep them from seeing the light of the gospel of the glory of Christ, who is the likeness of God' (2 Corinthians 4:4). When he expresses himself thus, Paul recalls the light from heaven which illuminated his own spiritual darkness – 'the light of the knowledge of the glory of God in the face of Christ' (2 Corinthians 4:6). What was it that Paul saw on the Damascus road? His own account is that he saw 'Jesus our Lord' (1 Corinthians 9:1). But in what form did he see him? Over six hundred years earlier, the prophet Ezekiel received the call to his life-ministry in a vision of God, and when he tried to describe that vision he strained the resources of human language to the limit. He saw the likeness of the throne of glory, he says, and above it 'was a likeness as it were of a human form' (Ezekiel 1:26). Paul too saw a glorified human figure, but the man who appeared to Paul gave himself a name: 'I am Jesus', he said (Acts 9:5). From then on Paul knew Jesus to be 'the image of the invisible God' (Colossians 1:15).

Incarnation

Thus, whether Jesus is called the word, the wisdom, the image or the glory of God, what is implied is that he is the self-expression of God, God revealed in a real human life. And what is this but incarnation?

God, who had revealed himself to the world in many ways before the coming of Christ, revealed himself perfectly then by being embodied in a particular man. There was nothing unreal or 'phoney' about Jesus' humanity: he was born, he grew up through childhood to manhood, he died. There was a line of thought in the first century AD which resisted the idea that God could involve himself in human existence or with the material universe to the degree envisaged by the doctrine of incarnation. Probably John, in insisting so uncompromisingly that in Jesus the eternal Word 'became flesh', was concerned to refute some who maintained that his humanity was more apparent than real. When one of the later documents of the

New Testament emphasises that Jesus 'came by water and blood . . . not with the water only but with the water and the blood' (1 John 5:6), the writer seems to have in view an idea, current in his day, that the divine being came upon the man Jesus when he was baptised in the Jordan and gave him the power to accomplish his mighty works, but left him before his death; and he aims to rule this idea out of court. Such an idea was totally subversive of the Christian gospel.

Jesus was exposed throughout his life to the same trials and tribulations as other human beings have to endure; he experienced the same temptations as we experience. Yet he resisted them successfully; he remained free from sin. And in the life as well as the teaching of this man, who was bone of our bone and flesh of our flesh, God has made himself known more completely than in any other way. As the eternal word of God was God's agent in self-revelation, Jesus has perfectly revealed the Father. As God in earlier days sent his word for the deliverance of those who were in desperate straits, the good news about Jesus assures us that 'the Father has sent his Son as the Saviour of the world' (1 John 4:14). As it was 'by the word of the Lord' that the universe was created, so Jesus is the divinely appointed agent for bringing the new creation into being, first in human life and then on a universal scale. More than that: Jesus by his rising from the dead is the head and first fruits of the new creation; he has led the way and his people follow.

In recent years a succession of monographs and symposia has been published, discussing whether or not incarnation is an acceptable 'model' today for conveying the way in which Jesus revealed God, and continues to reveal him. It would be difficult to find a model more acceptable or more adequate. If the other New Testament theologians do not use it expressly in the way John does, when he affirms that 'the Word became flesh', that is nevertheless what their testimony amounts to. In the humanity of Jesus the invisible and everlasting God is 'enfleshed'.

When we use language of this kind, we admittedly point to an act of God of the highest order. But if we view the Bible as a whole, we may see that God had this incarnation in view when he created humanity in his own image. Our Lord's virginal conception, which itself involved a creative miracle, is not to be confused with the incarnation; it was but the means by which the incarnation was effected.

We cannot, and indeed we would not, banish the element of mystery from this fundamental article of the Christian faith. The note of mystery was caught wonderfully well by Sir John Betjeman in the closing lines of his poem *Christmas*:

> And is it true? And is it true?
> This most tremendous tale of all . . . ?

There are some truths, and this is one of them, which are more adequately expressed in a few lines of poetry than in volumes of theological prose. An early Christian poet, whose words are quoted in the New Testament (1 Timothy 3:16), celebrated 'the mystery of our religion' thus:

> He was manifested in flesh,
>   vindicated in spirit;
> He appeared to angels,
>   was proclaimed among the nations;
> He was believed on in the world,
>   was taken up in glory.[2]

Chapter
17

The Savior of the World

Jesus and non-Jews

It is only in the writings of John that 'the Saviour of the world' appears in the New Testament as a designation of Jesus. The thought which is expressed by this designation, however, is plainly to be found throughout the New Testament.

'The Father has sent his Son as the Saviour of the world' is a Christian confession, concisely stated in 1 John 4:14. It is couched in characteristically Johannine language, but it is to much the same effect as the confession of 1 Timothy 1:15: 'Christ Jesus came into the world to save sinners.'

In the composition of his Gospel John combines an unfading memory of the events of Jesus' ministry with the insights gleaned from many decades' mature reflection on their significance – reflection in which he experienced the fulfilment of Jesus' promise to his disciples that, after his departure, the Spirit of truth would remind them of what he had told them and make its meaning plain to them. Some of these insights are compressed into short sentences: 'God did not send the Son into the world to judge the world, but that the world might be saved through him' (John 3:17). This is in line with Jesus' own statement, according to this Gospel: 'I did not come to judge the world but to save the world' (John 12:47). By his own claim, then, and by the testimony of the evangelist, he is the Saviour of the world. But on the one occasion when that precise title occurs in John's Gospel, it is placed on the lips of the men of Sychar, a Samaritan community, as they

say to the woman who told them of her remarkable conversation with Jesus at Jacob's well, 'It is no longer because of
your words that we believe, for we have heard for ourselves,
and we know that this is indeed the Saviour of the world'
(John 4:42).

Even if the evangelist is transposing the Samaritans' words
into his own idiom, it is significant and appropriate that he
should ascribe them to Samaritans. For the Samaritans were
not Jesus' own people. Although they traced their descent
from Abraham, Isaac and Jacob, and worshipped the God of
Israel according to the law of Moses, they were regarded by
the Jews as outsiders. When, in Acts 1:8, the risen Lord
commissions his apostles to carry their testimony 'to the end
of the earth', Samaria is the first non-Jewish region where
they are to witness. A Saviour preached to Jews only might be
a Saviour available for Jews only, but a Saviour preached to
Samaritans was a Saviour for non-Jews and therefore, by
implication, a Saviour for the world.

There is a widespread impression that the ministry of the
historical Jesus was strictly and deliberately confined to Jews,
in such a way that the extension of the good news to non-Jews
is excluded from his purview. This impression arises from a
number of gospel texts, most (though not all) of which belong
to Matthew's record. For example, when Jesus sent the
twelve apostles out to carry to every Jewish community in
Galilee the good news that the kingdom of God had come
near, he told them to 'Go nowhere among the Gentiles, and
enter no town of the Samaritans, but go rather to the lost
sheep of the house of Israel' (Matthew 10:5,6). The time was
short; they would scarcely succeed in covering all the Jewish
communities.[1]

The expression 'the lost sheep of the house of Israel' is
echoed in Matthew's account of the unforthcoming response
which Jesus made to the Canaanite woman's plea for aid
to her demon-possessed daughter: 'I was sent only to the
lost sheep of the house of Israel' (Matthew 15:24).[2] A negative attitude to Gentiles has also been discerned in Jesus'
direction to his disciples that the obstinate brother who

refuses even to 'hear the church' must be treated 'as a Gentile and a tax collector' (Matthew 18:17).[3]

On the other hand, this same Gospel of Matthew makes an addition of its own to the parable of the vineyard, in which Jesus warns the Jewish authorities that the kingdom of God will be taken away from them 'and given to a nation producing the fruits appropriate to it' (Matthew 21:43) – presumably to the Gentile church. It makes a similar addition to the story of the healing of the centurion's servant: after commending this Gentile for a measure of faith which he had not found among Israelites, Jesus goes on: 'I tell you, many will come from east and west and sit at table with Abraham, Isaac and Jacob in the kingdom of heaven, while the sons of the kingdom will be thrown into outer darkness; there men will weep and gnash their teeth' (Matthew 8:11,12).

Some readers have found such a contradiction between the restrictive and the comprehensive sayings that they feel obliged to dismiss one set as not authentic. For example, Dr Geza Vermes refers to Jesus' restrictive charge to the twelve and his discouraging reply to the Canaanite woman and asks, 'However did the evangelists manage to record such sayings as these, and at the same time attribute to Jesus the view that the Gentiles were soon to displace "the sons of the kingdom", the Jews, as the elect of God?'[4] His own answer is that the exclusive sayings are utterances of the historical Jesus, while those which express a more comprehensive spirit are due to the 'radical transformation' which deflected the original bias of Jesus' ministry as a result of Paul's Gentile apostleship. But if his question were put to Matthew, the answer would be that the exclusive sayings are temporary in character, related to the circumstances of Jesus' Galilaean ministry, while the more comprehensive sayings look forward to the time after his death, when the restrictions would be lifted. John in his Gospel takes exactly the same line. According to him, Jesus, who came as the good shepherd to call his own sheep by name out of the Jewish fold, went on to say, 'And I have other sheep, that are not of this fold; I must bring them also, and they will heed my voice. So there shall be one flock, one shepherd' (John 10:16). If it is not made plain in those words that the 'other sheep', the Gentile believers, would be brought into the flock of the good shepherd after his death, that is explicitly said in the account of the Greek visitors who sought an interview with him in Jerusalem during Holy Week. Jesus was reticent in his response to their request, but he added: 'When I am lifted up from the earth I will draw to myself all without distinction' (John 12:32). The Johannine expression 'to be lifted up' covers both Jesus' crucifixion and his exaltation.

Luke's Gospel does not contain Matthew's restrictive utterances, but it does contain some of the same comprehensive utterances, like the prediction of people coming from all directions to enjoy the banquet in the kingdom of God, while some who were first invited will find themselves shut out because they despised the invitation (Luke 13:28–30). As for Mark, the earliest of the evangelists, he reports Jesus as saying that, within a generation from the time of speaking, the gospel is to be proclaimed 'to all nations' (Mark 13:10). It is in keeping with this that Paul, apostle to the Gentiles, describes his commission as bringing about the obedience that springs from faith in Christ 'among all the nations' (Romans 1:5). Paul knows that the good news is presented 'to the Jew first and (then) also to the Greek' – that is, the Gentile (Romans 1:16) – and he shows, as he develops his argument, that its extension to Gentiles depends on Christ's abolishing by his death the barrier that previously stood between Jews and Gentiles. To ascribe the more comprehensive language of the Gospels to the influence of Paul's Gentile apostleship may overlook the fact that Paul was not the only, nor even the first, Christian missionary to the Gentiles in the New Testament age, though he was incomparably the greatest.

If, then, we find the four evangelists in their various ways, together with Paul (and other New Testament writers who might be mentioned), agreeing in this insight – that the ministry of Jesus was mostly confined to Jews before his death, but was intended to reach out to Gentiles after his death – it is a reasonable inference that their agreement derives from the mind of Christ. When Matthew and Luke tell how the risen Lord appeared to his disciples and recommissioned them, appointing them as his emissaries to 'all nations' (Matthew 28:19,20; Luke 24:47; Acts 1:8), there is no good ground for treating their account as an invention, or as the reading back of a later development into an earlier situation.

But if the disciples were commissioned to carry the good news to the Gentiles after their master's resurrection, why were they so slow and reluctant to undertake this part of their commission? Partly because witnessing to their fellow-Jews was a full time exercise; besides, it was easier witnessing to people with whom they had so much in common than to people with whom it was difficult to establish a suitable point of contact. Again, many of them would take it for granted that, if Gentiles were to be brought into the community of believers, this involved their becoming Jewish proselytes – submitting to circumcision and the Jewish law. One of the twelve apostles, Peter, is said to have made a breach with tradition several years after the resurrection of Christ by accepting an invitation to visit a Gentile and receive his hospitality, after which he preached the gospel to him and his family and baptised them without saying anything about circumcision or the obligation to keep the Jewish law. But it required a special revelation from the Lord to persuade Peter to violate ancestral tabus. When once he had done so, indeed, he recognised that he was actually fulfilling Jesus' commission; but he met with strong disapproval from his colleagues when they heard what he had done. The practical logic of Jesus' instructions takes a long time to be grasped, even today, by some for whom they are intended.

'The world' in the writings of John

On the lips of the people of Sychar the designation of Jesus as Saviour of the world would mean that he was the Saviour for Samaritans as well as for Jews. But in reporting this

John intends the designation to emphasise that he is also the Saviour for Gentiles.

It is striking that John should be the writer to speak of Jesus as the Saviour of the world, because there is a curious ambivalence in John's references to 'the world'. On the one hand, the world is opposed to God, it does not know God, it lies in the power of the evil one, who is 'the ruler of this world'. The disciples, whom the Father has given to the Son 'out of the world', live in the world but are no longer 'of the world', and the world therefore hates them, as it hated their master (John 17:6,11,14). Yet the world is not written off as beyond hope. If Jesus sends his disciples into the world, as the Father sent him (John 17:18), that sending is with a view to the world's salvation. Estranged as it is, the world is the object of the Father's love: if God sent his Son into the world 'that the world might be saved through him' (John 3:17), that is the measure of his love for the world. The Son sacrifices himself 'for the life of the world' (John 6:51); by his death the evil ruler of this world is dethroned (John 12:31). The Son's presence in the world precipitates a division between those who respond to him and those who refuse him; in this sense it is 'for judgment' that he came into the world (John 9:39). Yet this judgment is the self-judgment of those who refuse him: so far as the prime purpose of his coming into the world is concerned, it was not 'to judge the world, but to save the world' (John 12:47).[5]

John expresses all this in his own distinctive idiom, but his aim throughout is to set forth the permanent and universal significance of the life and work of Christ, to interpret the mind of Christ.

At the beginning of John's record John the Baptist hails Jesus as 'the Lamb of God, who takes away the sin of the world' (John 1:29). Jesus, in other words, is the universal sin-offering. Similarly, in 1 John 2:2, Jesus is said to be 'the atonement for our sins, and not for ours only, but also for the whole world'. He who is the personal Saviour of each believer is also, in Charles Wesley's phrase, 'the general Saviour of mankind' – the Saviour of the human race as such. Believers in him, even when they form a tiny minority (as they did in most places in New Testament times), are the first fruits of a gospel harvest surpassing all imagination in its abundance. It is not the evil power, but the crucified and risen Jesus, who is the rightful and final ruler of the world – and here we may supplement John's testimony with Paul's, according to which 'the creation itself will be set free from its bondage to decay and obtain the glorious liberty of the children of God' (Romans 8:21). But the liberation of creation itself (however that may be envisaged), like the liberation of the children of God, is the fruit of the redemptive work of Christ – a work accomplished on earth, in historical time, but eternally powerful throughout the universe of God.

'No other name'

However restricted Jesus' ministry may have been before his death, his claim to be the Saviour of the world was quickly vindicated in the decades immediately following. According to Luke 12:50, he spoke during his ministry of a 'baptism' which he had to undergo (by which he meant his death) – 'and how hampered I am', he said, 'until the ordeal is past!' But once the ordeal was past, the message of Jesus was not long in finding as much acceptance among non-Jews as among Jews – more acceptance, indeed, after the first generation. The first communication of his message to non-Jews was the work of anonymous Christians, who without any special commissioning began to share the good news with their Gentile neighbours. The place where they started to do this was Antioch, a great city in the north of Syria. The Gentiles with whom they shared the good news took to it like ducks to water: this was the very message they had been waiting for, the very thing that met their need. It was among those people, at Antioch, that the disciples of Jesus first came to be called Christians.

Since that time, in one generation after another and progressively in all parts of the world, men, women and children who have heard the story of Jesus have recognised in it

something completely suited to their condition and have
welcomed Jesus as their all-sufficient Lord and deliverer.
There is no cultural climate in which Jesus cannot make
himself at home, which he cannot claim for himself, where his
saving grace and power cannot be experienced. His message
of liberation is for the whole human family.

We should not disparage the founders of any of the great
world-religions, but it is the simple truth that none of them is
entitled to be called the Saviour of the world. Jesus alone
bears this designation, and 'there is salvation in no one else,
for there is no other name under heaven given among men by
which we must be saved' (Acts 4:12).

Chapter
18

The Coming One

'Are you the coming one?'

'The coming one' – he who is coming or he who is to come – is not exactly a title of Jesus. Yet it is an expression applied to him often enough, with reference either to his historical coming into the world or to his second coming or indeed (at times) to his repeated comings.

On the occasion when John the Baptist, imprisoned by Herod Antipas, sent two messengers to interview Jesus and to investigate and report on his activities, the question which they were instructed to put to him was 'Are you the coming one, or must we look for someone else?' (Matthew 11:3; Luke 7:20). John, in the days of his freedom, had announced that he was preparing the way for one 'stronger' than himself, who would administer a judgment of wind and fire. He had a clear idea in his mind of the kind of person this 'coming one' would be, and the kind of work he would do, and he was no longer so sure as he had once been that Jesus conformed to that idea.

It is plain that, when John began his baptismal ministry, there were many views abroad about one or more figures whose appearance, shortly expected, would signal the winding up of the current age and the inauguration of a new age. Some attempts were made to identify John himself with one or another of those figures. When he denied that he was the Messiah, he was asked, 'Are you Elijah?' – for one of the later prophets had foretold how God would send Elijah back to earth (from which he had been caught up in a whirlwind centuries before) to discharge a reconciling ministry before 'the great and terrible day of the Lord' (Malachi 4:5,6). 'No', said John. 'Well, then, are you the prophet?' John had no need to ask 'Which prophet?' He knew that his questioners had in mind the prophet of whom Moses spoke when he told the people, 'The Lord your God will raise up for you a prophet like me' (Deuteronomy 18:15). But he denied that he was that prophet. He would identify himself with none of these figures of popular expectation; he was simply the 'voice' calling on men and women to 'prepare the way of the Lord' (as it is put in Isaiah 40:3), to make ready for his imminent intervention.[1]

Naturally, as attempts had been made to identify John with one or another of those expected figures, similar attempts were made with regard to Jesus. Some of those attempts were reviewed by Jesus' disciples when he asked them at Caesarea Philippi, 'Who do people say I am?'

In those days there were three outstanding personages who were widely expected to appear in Israel – a great king (a second David), a great priest (a second Aaron), and a great prophet (a second Moses). In one of the documents of the Qumran community it is laid down that the community shall live according to specified rules 'until the rise of a prophet and the anointed ones of Aaron of Israel'. The 'prophet' (as is shown by other Qumran texts) is the prophet like Moses, the 'anointed one of Aaron' is a high priest of Aaron's line (a priestly Messiah) and the 'anointed one of Israel' is to be identified with the son of David, a conquering king (a lay Messiah).[2]

The coming king

Jesus, as we have seen, did not disclaim the title 'son of David' when it was given to him, but he laid no weight on his descent from David. If the title Messiah conjured up in people's minds the picture of a warrior-king like David, then it was better not to use it. For there could hardly be a greater contrast than that between David's career and the career of 'great David's greater Son'. On the occasion when the high priest asked Jesus point-blank whether or not he was the Messiah, he qualified his affirmative reply immediately by adding words expressing what he really claimed for himself.

The word Messiah is based on the Hebrew word meaning 'anointed'; the term Christ comes from the Greek word which bears the same meaning. David and the other kings of Israel were literally anointed with oil when they were invested with royal authority. Jesus was anointed for his messianic role when the Spirit of God came upon him as he emerged from the Jordan after being baptised by John. When, according to Luke's narrative, Jesus in the synagogue of Nazareth read the opening clauses of Isaiah 61, 'The Spirit of the Lord is upon me, because he has anointed me . . .' (Luke 4:18), it was to his baptism that he referred. To the same effect Peter referred to Jesus' baptism when he preached the gospel for the first time to a Gentile audience in the house of Cornelius at Caesarea and told how 'God anointed Jesus of Nazareth with the Holy Spirit and with power' (Acts 10:38).

So, when Christians speak of Jesus as the Messiah or the Christ, they forget the military and political associations of royal anointing in Old Testament times, and fill those terms with the meaning which Jesus gave them by being the person he was and doing the things he did. When we say 'Jesus is the Christ', it is the name Jesus that gives meaning to the term Christ, not the other way round. Jesus' kingly authority was vindicated on the cross; when Christians sing,

> Our great foe is baffled;
> Christ Jesus is King!

they sing of the victory which he has won by death and resurrection.

The coming priest

There was another functionary in ancient Israel who was installed in office by being anointed with oil. That was the high priest, the successor of Aaron. The great priest whom the Qumran community expected to arise at the end of the current age was therefore called 'the anointed one of Aaron'. This was a role which Jesus could never fill, for a very simple reason. The priests of Aaron's line belonged to the tribe of Levi; Jesus belonged to the tribe of Judah. In no way could he be recognised as the Aaronic high priest.

There is, however, one document in the New Testament which does expressly portray Jesus as his people's high priest, ministering on their behalf in the heavenly sanctuary on the basis of one perfect sacrifice which he presented once for all when he offered up his own life. That document is the letter to the Hebrews. But when the unidentified author of that work seeks Old Testament authority for portraying Jesus as high priest, he finds it not in the Aaronic priesthood but in an ancient oracle where God swears a mighty oath to the Messiah of David's line (who belonged to the tribe of Judah): 'You are a priest for ever after the order of Melchizedek' (Psalm 110:4). Melchizedek was priest-king in Jerusalem back in the days of Abraham, and the writer to the Hebrews argues that at one point after another Melchizedek's priesthood was far more august and effective than Aaron's, and that it has found its complete fulfilment in Jesus.

Like Aaron and his successors, Jesus is represented in the letter to the Hebrews as an anointed high priest, but again, his anointing is not carried out literally, with specially blended oil, but spiritually. A reference to Jesus' anointing is found in one of the royal psalms, where the Messiah is addressed thus (Psalm 45:7):

> You love righteousness and hate wickedness;
> therefore God, your God, has anointed you
> with the oil of gladness above your companions.[3]

The other New Testament writers do not give Jesus the designation 'high priest', but when Paul speaks of him as interceding for his people in the presence of God (Romans 8:34) and John calls him our 'advocate with the Father' (1 John 2:1), they express in other terms something of what the writer to the Hebrews means by calling him his people's high priest.

The coming prophet

When we turn to the expected prophet like Moses, here is a figure whose realisation in Jesus is direct and unambiguous. When Moses told the Israelites that God would raise up a prophet for them when he wished to communicate his will to them, he added: 'you must listen to him' (Deuteronomy 18:15). So far as Moses' words were concerned, the promise might have been fulfilled in any generation after his. But the Israelites had long to wait before a comparable prophet arose from their midst. Moses' obituary tribute at the end of the book of Deuteronomy, obviously composed a considerable time after Moses' death, says, 'There has not risen since in Israel a prophet like Moses, whom the Lord knew face to face.'[4] As late as the time of the Qumran community, at the end of the pre-Christian era, the people were still waiting for such a prophet.

Some of Jesus' contemporaries were quick to recognise in him the prophet of whom Moses spoke. When he fed the multitude in the wilderness, when in the temple court he called those who were thirsty to come to him and drink, some of the people said, 'This is indeed the prophet!' (John 6:14; 7:40). They meant the prophet like Moses, for they remembered how their ancestors in the wilderness, under the leadership of Moses, had been fed with bread from heaven (the manna) and refreshed with water from the rock.

When, at Jesus' transfiguration, the disciples who were present heard the heavenly voice say, 'This is my beloved

Son; listen to him' (Mark 9:7), those last words clearly
identified Jesus with the coming prophet of whom Moses had
said, 'you must listen to him.' Similarly, on two occasions in
the Acts of the Apostles Moses' words about the coming
prophet are quoted and applied to Jesus – once by Peter and
once by Stephen (Acts 3:22,23; 7:37).

The word 'prophet' means 'spokesman'. Moses was the
greatest of God's spokesmen before the coming of Jesus. Now
in Jesus God has sent his perfect spokesman. He alone can
fully satisfy the terms of Moses' prophecy; he is the one to
whom all must listen.

He who came will come again

Jesus, then, was hailed in various ways as the coming one, and
he is proclaimed in the gospel as the one who came – king,
priest and prophet. But the gospel proclaims him not only as
the one who came – 'came into the world to save sinners' – but
also as the one who continues to come in the present and will
come climactically in the future. 'Yet a little while', says the
writer to the Hebrews (expressing a common New Testament
outlook), 'and the coming one will come; he will make no
delay' (Hebrews 10:37).

When Jesus faced the high priest's court of inquiry, he told
his judges that they had not yet seen the last of him: they
would see him again 'coming with the clouds of heaven'. As
we have said above, the clouds of heaven convey the idea of
the divine presence. The reference may be not just to one
single coming at the end of time but to repeated manifes-
tations of Jesus' presence and power in the course of world
history as well as in the experience of his people. It is an
essential element in the Christian message that, because of his
sacrifice and death, Jesus is the Lord both of history and of
destiny. In the language of the book of Revelation, he is 'the
first and the last, the living one', the one 'who was and is, the
coming one'.[5] Because he is the coming one, there is nothing
static about him; he is a dynamic presence in human life,

coming when least expected and leading towards further horizons in the unfolding of God's purpose.

According to John's Gospel, Jesus told his disciples in the upper room, a few hours before his arrest, that he was going to leave them but that he would return to them. His returning would take more forms than one. It would be, in one form, a returning beyond their present life: 'when I go and prepare a place for you, I will come again and will take you to myself, that where I am you may be also' (John 14:3). But in another form it would be a returning within their present life: 'I will not leave you desolate (orphans); I will come to you' (John 14:18). This last promise would be fulfilled by the sending of the Paraclete, the Holy Spirit, Jesus' other self, to be their constant helper, teacher and guide and to make his personal presence continuously real to them. Yet not even the sending of the Paraclete exhausted the fulfilment of the promise: by bringing his followers into the fellowship of love which united the Father and the Son, Jesus would make them more immediately conscious of his companionship, if possible, than they had been when he was visibly and audibly present with them.[6]

The goal of history

A nineteenth-century English poet expressed a confidence more characteristic of his own age than of ours in the lines:

Yet I doubt not thro' the ages one increasing purpose runs,
And the thoughts of men are widen'd with the process of the suns.[7]

It was no distinctively Christian insight that he voiced. But the phrase 'one increasing purpose' can sum up very well the Christian perspective on the course of time. This is how that perspective is put in one remarkable passage in the New Testament. 'In all his wisdom and insight God did what he had purposed, and made known to us the secret plan he had already decided to complete by means of Christ. This plan, which God will complete when the time is right, is to bring all creation together, everything in heaven and on earth, with Christ as head' (Ephesians 1:8–10, Good News Bible). The world of space and time, that is, with all its conflicting elements, will ultimately be reconciled and unified under the headship of Christ. The reconciling process inaugurated by his death on the cross – the reconciliation of men and women to God and the reconciliation of antagonistic divisions within the human family – is to be consummated in the final reconciliation when the universe is brought into a unity in Christ. Nothing less than this is implied when the crucified one is acknowledged to be Lord of all.

The righteous judge

Jesus, who did not come to judge the world but to save the world, nevertheless by his coming initiated a judgment in which men and women declared themselves either for him or against him. And this self-judgment on their part would be the basis of their judgment at the last assize.

On one occasion he drew a vivid word-picture of the advent of the Son of Man, when he would be seated on his glorious throne, and all the nations would be brought before him for judgment. He would separate the righteous from the unrighteous, 'as a shepherd separates the sheep from the goats', and would hand down the appropriate rewards and penalties to both groups. Members of both groups would be surprised by his adjudication, for it would not conform to general courtroom practice. The criterion for judgment would be their treatment of the poor, the weak, the oppressed and the underprivileged. These are counted by the Son of Man as his brothers and sisters, and to those whom he judges he says, 'In doing it to them, you have done it to me' (Matthew 25:31–46).

This is Jesus' application of the judgment scene in the book of Daniel, where a human figure ('one like a son of man') receives royal and judicial authority from God.[8] Plainly the Son of Man of whom Jesus spoke is to be identified with himself. This is how his words were understood by his followers after his death and resurrection. Peter announced in the house of Cornelius that Jesus 'is the one ordained by God to be judge of the living and the dead' (Acts 10:42). Paul told the court of the Areopagus at Athens that God 'has fixed a day on which he will judge the world in righteousness by a man whom he has appointed, and of this he has given assurance to all men by raising him from the dead' (Acts 17:31). In his letter to the Christians of Rome he refers similarly to 'that day when, according to my gospel, God will judge the hidden motives of human beings through Christ Jesus' (Romans 2:16). Later in the same letter he says, 'we shall all stand before the judgment seat of God' (Romans 14:10), but when he speaks of the same prospect in 2 Corinthians 5:10 he says, 'we must all appear before the judgment seat of Christ'. These are not two judgment seats but one: it is through Christ's agency that God will carry out his work of judgment, just as it was through Christ's agency that he carried out his work of creation.

So Christians still sing to Christ in the *Te Deum*, 'We believe that thou shalt come to be our judge.' But this end-time judgment brings to a head the ongoing judgment which works itself out in generation after generation. 'The history of the world is the judgment of the world', said the German poet Schiller. And if Christ is the divinely appointed judge of the human race, this tells us something about the nature and principles of his judgment. It is in accordance with his character, his teaching and his life that the ultimate assessment will be made. The Jesus of history insisted that his teaching provided the only firm foundation for human life. 'Whoever hears my words *and acts accordingly*', he said, 'is like a man building a house, who dug deep and laid the foundation on rock. When a flood arose, the stream broke against that house and could not shake it, because it had been well built. But whoever hears my words *and takes no action* is like a man who built a house on the ground without a foundation. When the stream broke against it, it collapsed immediately, in utter ruin' (Luke 6:47–49).

The truth of this manifests itself repeatedly in the history of individuals and communities. Jesus' words indicate clearly enough what the criterion in the final judgment will be. There is nothing arbitrary about it: the judgment inheres in the character of the persons who are judged and in the nature of their actions.

John in his Gospel does not use the pictorial language of the other evangelists when he speaks of judgment. Jesus, he says, is the one to whom the Father has given authority to execute judgment. Already in his earthly ministry men and women have chosen life or death according to their response to him and his teaching; the same principle will operate in the last judgment. Of anyone who has rejected him or his teaching, Jesus says, 'it is the word that I have spoken that will judge him at the last day' (John 12:48).

The raising of the dead

To raise the dead to life, in Jewish, Christian and Muslim teaching, is the prerogative of God. According to the New Testament, this prerogative (like the prerogative of passing final judgment) is one which the Father shares with the Son. It is fitting that the one whom God has already raised from the dead should be the one through whom he will raise others. The Son's exercise of his delegated authority to raise the dead is presented in the Gospel of John on two levels: 'The hour is coming', says Jesus, 'indeed, it is already here, when the dead will hear the voice of the Son of God, and those who hear will live' (John 5:25). This refers to the life-giving message of the gospel, to which the divine command through an Old Testament prophet might be compared: 'Incline your ear, and come to me; hear, that your soul may live' (Isaiah 55:3). But in the same context of John's record Jesus continues, 'the hour is coming when all who are in the tombs will hear his voice and come forth, those who have done good, to the resurrection of life, and those who have done evil, to the resurrection of judgment' (John 5:28,29).

This final raising of the dead – more particularly of those who have died believing in him – is closely associated in the New Testament with Christ's second coming. 'We look for the Saviour', says Paul, 'who will change the body of our humiliation and transform it to be like his body of glory' (Philippians 3:20,21). This transformation is their participating in Christ's own resurrection; it is the completion of the process which was inaugurated when he was raised from the dead. With regard to the resurrection of the dead Paul says in another letter, 'every one will be raised in the proper order: Christ the firstfruits; afterwards, at his coming, the people of Christ' (1 Corinthians 15:23). That is to say, the resurrection of Christ's people is the final harvest of which his own resurrection was the first stage – the presentation of the first fruits, the first ripe sheaf, whose dedication to God consecrated the whole of the ensuing crop.

Since Christ's resurrection provides the precedent, the resurrection of his people is no mere revival of corpses to a renewal of bodily life as we know it at present; it is a sharing of that new order of existence, 'eternal life', which Christ inaugurated when he rose from the dead. As with final judgment, so final resurrection is the consummation of something that is already a matter of experience. Those who are 'in Christ' live here and now in the enjoyment of his fellowship and share in the power of his risen life. This power is made good to them by the Spirit of Christ, who is at work within his people. But this Spirit is also the pledge of immortality – the pledge of their participation in Christ's immortality. It is in prospect of his resurrection that the Jesus of John's Gospel says to his disciples, 'because I live, you will live also' (John 14:19). If Christ rose from the dead and is alive for evermore, those who live 'in him' in this earthly existence will not be separated from him when their earthly existence comes to an end. For them, in Paul's words, to depart this life is to be 'with Christ, which is far better' (Philippians 1:23). As the body is our means of communication with our present environment, so a means of communication with the new environment is even now being prepared – 'a house not made with hands, eternal in the heavens' (2 Corinthians 5:1) – so that no conscious hiatus intervenes between this mortal life and that immortal life for those who are united to Christ by faith. Whatever form their investiture with glory at Christ's advent may take, it can only be the confirmation of a reality which is already theirs.

Those Christians, then, who look for the coming of Christ do not look for it so much for their own sake as for his sake and the world's. Already, on this earth where Jesus was disowned and put to death, he is confessed as Lord by hundreds of millions. This confession will achieve its climax when 'The kingdom of the world has become the kingdom of our Lord and of his Christ, and he shall reign for ever and ever' (Revelation 11:15), when the way of Jesus becomes the rule of life for all.

Christ coming and to come

But this climax involves not only the universal acceptance of the way of Jesus and his universal acknowledgment as Lord; it involves above all the manifestation of the personal Christ. The personal Christ who is always 'at hand' when he is most needed is yet to be revealed in the fullness of his glory – that is to say, his fullness of grace and truth.

One difficulty felt by many people today when they read the New Testament on this subject is that the writers apparently envisaged the final coming of Christ as close at hand – if not within their own lifetime. But they did not make dogmatic assertions about its timing, of a kind which could have been proved wrong by the course of time. They did not know when it would take place, and did not pretend that they knew. So, as time went on, their perspective changed, but not their doctrine or their hope. In this they were wiser than some Christians of a later date, who from time to time throughout the Christian era have committed themselves to public statements that Christ would come again in this or that year (if not

on this or that day) – only to be put out of countenance when
their confident predictions have failed to come true.

If John reports Jesus as saying to his disciples in the upper
room, 'I will come again', Matthew reports him as saying to
them after he rose from the dead, 'I am with you always, right
on to the end of time' (Matthew 28:20). If the end of time (a
concept difficult for our imagination to grasp) coincides with
his final coming, he is not absent from his people here and
now. The belief that he will 'come again with glory to judge
both the living and the dead' does not conflict with his ongoing
involvement in human life in the ages between his first coming
and his coming again. The close relation between his presence
now and his last advent was never (to my knowledge) more
aptly expressed than by John Henry Newman, a century and a
half ago:

> Up to Christ's coming in the flesh [he said] the course of
> things ran straight towards that end, nearing it by every
> step, but now, under the Gospel, that course has (if I may
> so speak) altered its direction, as regards His second com-
> ing, and runs, not towards the end, but along it, and on the
> brink of it; and is at all times equally near that great event,
> which, did it run towards it, it would at once run into.
> Christ, then, is ever at our doors; as near eighteen hundred
> years ago as now, and not nearer now than then; and not
> nearer when He comes than now.[9]

The present is his, for he is our eternal contemporary; but
the future also is his. And because it is his, it belongs to all
those who belong to him: they may greet one another with
'Brother, sister, the future is ours!' They know him as 'Christ
our life'; they know him also as 'Christ Jesus our hope' (1
Timothy 1:1).[10]

Chapter
19

Jesus Is Lord

Marana-tha

Marana-tha is an Aramaic phrase expressing a prayer: 'Our Lord, come!' It was one way in which Christians of the earliest age voiced their appreciation of Christ as the coming one. It occurs once in the New Testament: Paul uses it in the final greetings of one of his letters, as he bids his readers farewell (1 Corinthians 16:22). Its Greek equivalent appears more than once in the New Testament – for example, in the invocation 'Come, Lord Jesus!' near the end of the book of Revelation (Revelation 22:20).

In its original form *Marana-tha*, like the Aramaic *Abba* or the Hebrew *Hosanna*, *Amen* and *Hallelujah* (*Alleluya*), passed untranslated into the language of worship used by Greek-speaking churches (and in due course by churches speaking many other languages). Paul takes it for granted that the Greek-speaking Christians of Corinth will understand it, without his having to translate it for them when he uses it in a letter to them. Fifty years later, a manual of church order for the use of Greek-speaking Christians in Syria uses the phrase at the end of the thanksgiving which concludes the Lord's Supper:

> Let grace come and let this world pass away.
> Hosanna to the God of David!
> If any one is holy, let him come;
> if any one is not, let him repent.
> Marana-tha! Amen![1]

Evidently it was no more necessary to translate *Maran-tha* than it was to translate *Hosanna* or *Amen*. The invocation 'Our Lord, come!' was specially appropriate for the supper in which Christians realised the presence of their risen Lord and were taught to 'proclaim the Lord's death until he comes' (1 Corinthians 11:26).

The word *mar* ('lord') had a wide range of meaning. In some Aramaic documents dating from shortly before the Christian era it occurs as an equivalent of such divine names as *Shaddai* ('the Almighty') or *Yahweh* (the personal name of the God of Israel). At the other end of the scale it was an ordinary title of courtesy for any man; it has, for example, been taken over into modern Hebrew as the counterpart to the English 'Mr'.

Since the form *Marana-tha* was addressed to the risen Christ in the context of worship, a sense nearer the divine end of the scale of meaning was probably intended.

Lord in resurrection

What is true of the Aramaic form is equally true of the Greek word *kyrios*, used repeatedly in the New Testament with reference to Jesus, sometimes preceding his name, sometimes as a substitute for his name. When early Christians said 'Jesus is Lord' (*kyrios Iēsous*), they used the word in its most exalted sense. That is why they refused to say 'Caesar is Lord'. It is not that they refused to honour the Roman Emperor; on the contrary, they made a special point of honouring him. But they would not allow him to share an honour which, in their view, belonged to Christ alone. To say 'Caesar is Lord' from the later years of the first century AD onwards was to acknowledge his divinity, and this was something which Christians could not do. When the sovereign of the United Kingdom is a man, his Christian subjects may speak of 'our sovereign Lord the King' without being charged with disloyalty to Christ, who is the Lord of his people; but then no one supposes that when a British king is referred to in this way he is being honoured as divine. It was different for Christians in the Roman Empire.

Yet this Greek word, *kyrios*, had, and still has, the same wide range of meaning as the Aramaic *mar*, especially in the vocative case *kyrie* (the case used when someone is being addressed). To the man who orders a cup of coffee the Greek waiter will say, 'Immediately, *kyrie*', as he goes off to fulfil the order. If, having drunk his coffee, the man goes into a neighbouring church, he will hear the celebrant use the same word as he leads the congregation in the liturgy: *Kyrie eleison*, 'Lord have mercy (upon us)!' There must be some special reason for the sense in which the word is applied exclusively to Christ: 'Jesus is *kyrios*'. It is only by the power of the Holy Spirit, says Paul, that anyone can make this confession (1 Corinthians 12:3). To make this confession is to be assured of salvation: 'if you confess with your lips that Jesus is Lord (*kyrios*) and believe in your heart that God raised him from the dead, you will be saved' (Romans 10:9). The confession is outward, the belief is inward; but it is implied that 'Jesus is Lord' and 'God raised him from the dead' are two variant forms of one and the same confession. It is as the risen one, that is to say, that Jesus is Lord – or at least that he is known to be Lord in this highest of all senses.

Teacher and Lord

During his teaching ministry, according to the Gospels, Jesus was regularly called lord, master or teacher. In the Greek text a variety of words is used in this way – both *kyrios* and a few others. If we try to penetrate back to the Aramaic in which the words were actually spoken, two principal terms appear to have been used – *mar*, at which we have looked already, and *rabbi*. When Jesus said to his disciples in the upper room, 'You call me Teacher and Lord' (John 13:13), behind the evangelist's Greek we can discern the Aramic *rabbi* and *mar*. *Rabbi*, or the fuller form *Rabbuni* (as in Mark 10:51; John 20:16), was a term of respect given to a religious teacher.

Etymologically it means 'my great one' but, as usual, etymology has very little to do with the sense of a word. Jesus' friends and followers appear to have referred to him as 'the rabbi'. When Jesus arrived in Bethany after the death of Lazarus, Martha went to her sister Mary and said, 'The rabbi is here; he is calling for you' (John 11:28). The Greek word that John uses in telling the story means 'teacher'; it is not difficult to see *rabbi* behind it as the word originally spoken. When Jesus sent two of his disciples to a certain house in Jerusalem to prepare the Passover meal, he told them to say to the householder. 'The rabbi says, "Where is my guest room, where I am to eat the passover with my disciples?"' (Mark 14:14). Nicodemus, himself a leading teacher in Israel, approached Jesus with the words: 'Rabbi, we know that you are a teacher come from God' (John 3:2). It is not certain that by Jesus' time the title Rabbi had attained a technical sense (in which it was reserved for those who were regularly ordained); it was, in any case, in no technical sense that Nicodemus used it but as an expression of courtesy.

The word *kyrios*, especially in the vocative *kyrie*, was also used by way of courtesy by several people who spoke to Jesus. 'Sir, you have nothing to draw with', said the Samaritan woman when Jesus undertook to give her 'living water'; to her at that stage in the conversation he was nothing but a Jewish traveller, if a most unusual one (John 4:11). 'Sir, come down before my son dies', said the official of Capernaum who was anxious that Jesus should cure his desperately sick son (John 4:49).

The word has a more august sense when Elizabeth welcomes the virgin Mary as 'the mother of my Lord' (Luke 1:43), or when the angel of the Lord announces to the shepherds of Bethlehem the birth of 'a Saviour, who is Christ the Lord' – the anointed *kyrios* (Luke 2:11) – but then, the angel of the Lord would have superior knowledge.

As for the evangelists themselves, they do not usually refer to Jesus as 'the Lord' in narrating his deeds and words up to the time of his death. Luke indeed does so more frequently than the others; perhaps he wants to remind his readers that the one of whom he writes is now the risen and exalted one. In the Gospel of John Jesus is called 'the Lord' three times before his death; it is remarkable that these three instances (John 4:1; 6:23; 11:2) come in passages which are widely recognised on other grounds as due to an editor rather than to the evangelist himself.

But in the resurrection narratives of the Gospels Jesus is called 'the Lord' or 'my Lord' much more freely. This is consistent with Peter's declaration on the day of Pentecost that, by raising him from the dead and exalting him to his right hand, God has made the crucified Jesus 'both Lord and Christ' (Acts 2:36). In a parallel statement Paul speaks of Jesus as being 'designated Son of God in power . . . by his resurrection' (Romans 1:4). If the resurrection made no difference to his identity, it made a difference to the promulgation and recognition of his identity.

'The Lord said to my Lord'

Peter based his declaration that the crucified Jesus was now 'both Lord and Christ' on the opening words of Psalm 110: 'The Lord says to my Lord, "Sit at my right hand . . ."' This oracle, in its original setting, was addressed by the God of Israel to the king of Israel, the Lord's anointed. As Peter applies the oracle, 'the Lord' who speaks is God the Father; 'my Lord' to whom he speaks is his Son, the Messiah. This is in line with the interpretation put on these words by Jesus himself (Mark 12:35–37), when he asked the scribes how the one whom David referred to as 'my Lord' could at the same time be David's son (as they believed the Messiah to be). In the Hebrew text of the psalm there is a clear distinction between the speaker and the one spoken to, for two different words are used: 'An oracle of Yahweh to my *'ādôn*.' But when the Hebrew scriptures were translated from Hebrew into Greek, one and the same noun did service in both capacities: 'The *kyrios* said to my *kyrios*'. It is as *kyrios* that the risen Christ is invited to be enthroned at God's right hand: that is the point of Peter's declaration. But those who could read the scriptures in Greek only might be encouraged to equate the one *kyrios* with the other.

The name high over all

More than once we have referred to the hymn in praise of Christ's glory which is incorporated in Philippians 2:6–11.[2] It is particularly relevant to the subject we are now considering, and this time it would be well to reproduce it in full. The rendering is rather prosaic, but it tries to bring out the point of the hymn.

> He already shared the nature of God
>> but did not exploit his equality with God for his own
>>> advantage.
> Instead, he emptied himself and took the nature of a
>> servant:
> He was born as all human beings are.
> Revealed in human form, he humbled himself,
>> and pursued the path of obedience to the point of
> death – even death on the cross.

> Therefore God in turn has highly exalted him
>> and given him the name above every name,
> That at Jesus' name every knee should bend
>> in heaven, on earth, and in the underworld,
> And every tongue confess, 'Jesus Christ is Lord!' –
>> to God the Father's glory.[3]

It seems probable that this hymn was known in the churches of that early period (Philippians was written about AD 60) before Paul quoted it in his letter. But by quoting it, Paul made it his own. He weaves it into his argument, using the first of its two stanzas to reinforce his plea for humility and unselfish concern for others. These, he points out, were the qualities that Christ displayed, and they should characterise his people.

But it is the second stanza that claims our attention now. In response to Jesus' unreserved acceptance of a life of humble service, culminating in his vile and degrading death by crucifixion, God has bestowed unreserved honour on him. The hymn includes echoes of Isaiah 52:13, where it is said of the submissive Servant of the Lord that, after his rejection and suffering, 'he shall be exalted and lifted up, and shall be very high', and also of Isaiah 45:23, where the one true God swears by himself: 'To me every knee shall bend, every tongue make solemn confession.' But in the Christ-hymn it is this same God who decrees that every knee shall bend at *Jesus'* name and every tongue confess that Jesus Christ is *Lord*. It is this same God, moreover, who declares in that part of the book of Isaiah, 'I am the Lord, that is my name; my glory I give to no other' (Isaiah 42:8). But now he shares that glory with the crucified Jesus by exalting him to universal supremacy and bestowing on him the name which is above every name – his own incommunicable name, 'The Lord'. It is sometimes asked whether 'the name above every name' in the Christ-hymn is 'Jesus' or 'Lord'. It is both, because by divine decree the name 'Jesus' henceforth has the value of the name 'Lord' in the highest sense which that name can bear – the sense of the Hebrew *Yahweh*. Charles Wesley got it right (as he usually did) in his version of this part of the Christ-hymn:

> Jesus! the name high over all
> In hell, and earth, and sky.

The power of Jesus' name, before which disease and death fled during his ministry on earth, has been enhanced with his resurrection and enthronement:

> Angels and men before it fall,
> And devils fear and fly.

New Testament usage

The possibility was suggested above that when the words 'The Lord said to my Lord' were read in the Greek Bible by people who had no access to the Hebrew text (where two different nouns are used) they might have been encouraged to equate the one Lord with the other. But in the Christ-hymn it is not a matter of inadvertently equating them: it is deliberately affirmed that God has conferred his own name, with the unique dignity attaching to it, on Jesus. It might not be appropriate to reword 'Jesus Christ is Lord' as 'Jesus Christ is Yahweh'; but nothing less than this is involved.

This usage did not originate with Paul (if the Christ-hymn is pre-Pauline), but repeatedly he ascribes to Jesus Old Testament texts and phrases in which the word 'Lord' represents the Hebrew Yahweh. 'The day of the Lord' (the great day of judgment) in the Old Testament is the day of Yahweh; what Paul understood by it is shown by the way in which he calls it variously 'the day of the Lord', 'the day of the Lord Jesus', or 'the day of Christ'. In Joel 2:32, 'whoever calls on the name of the Lord will be saved', 'the Lord' is Yahweh; but when Paul quotes this passage in Romans 10:13 the context makes it plain that for him 'the Lord' is Jesus.

Other New Testament writers share this usage with Paul; they did not derive it from him. The writer to the Hebrews applies to Christ the words of Psalm 102:25, which were originally addressed to Yahweh. He knows what he is doing, for the Greek version which he quotes adds the word 'Lord' which is not present in the Hebrew text of this verse: 'Thou, Lord, didst found the earth in the beginning' (Hebrews 1:10).[4]

The words of Isaiah 8:13, 'The Lord of hosts, him you shall sanctify', were designed as a message of encouragement to the people of Jerusalem in the eighth century BC. In 1 Peter 3:15 they are taken up and applied as a message of encouragement to Christians exposed to persecution under the Roman Empire, but an interpretative word is significantly added: 'sanctify in your hearts *Christ* as Lord'.

John the Evangelist quotes words from Isaiah's inaugural vision and finds their fulfilment in the ministry of Jesus: 'Isaiah said this because he saw his glory and spoke of him' (John 12:40,41). That is to say, 'the Lord' whom Isaiah says he saw on that occasion (Isaiah 6:1) was Jesus. John's wording is akin to that of the Aramaic paraphrase or 'targum' of Isaiah 6:1: 'I saw the glory of the Lord'. It was *Jesus'* glory, John implies, that Isaiah saw.

When the Apocalypse calls Jesus 'Lord of lords and King of kings' (Revelation 17:14) or 'King of kings and Lord of lords' (Revelation 19:16), there may be an echo of Deuteronomy 10:17, 'the Lord your God is . . . Lord of lords', or of Daniel 2:47, where Nebuchadnezzar acknowledges that Daniel's God is 'God of gods and Lord of kings'. But that is not surprising in a book whose introductory vision can take the attributes of God, portrayed as the Ancient of Days in Daniel 7:9, and ascribe them to 'one like a son of man' (Revelation 1:13,14).

These New Testament writers, Paul and the others, were monotheistic Jews by upbringing and instinct. What possessed them to transfer to Jesus of Nazareth titles and activities which belonged to God alone? Nothing but the assurance that God himself had set them a precedent by so highly exalting Jesus. He had declared his good pleasure 'that all may honour the Son, even as they honour the Father' (John 5:23).

The ascription of such divine honours of Jesus cannot be put down to the New Testament writers' adoption of a strange technique of Old Testament interpretation. It must be put down rather to the impact made by the Jesus of history not only on those who saw and heard him and remained in his company during his ministry, but also on others who had never met him in this way but first came to know him as the risen Christ.

The confession 'Jesus is Lord' ascribes to him a degree of honour which cannot be surpassed: in saying that, we say all. 'Jesus is Lord' remains the sufficient Christian confession. But it carries with it the corollary on which he himself insisted:

that those who call him 'Lord' should do what he says (Luke 6:46).

Where Christian belief is concerned, then, it remains true since the days of the apostles that 'for us there is one God, the Father, from whom are all things and for whom we exist, and one Lord, Jesus Christ, through whom are all things and through whom we exist' (1 Corinthians 8:6).

Chapter
20

Jesus Christ the Same

'Jesus Christ is the same yesterday and today and for ever.' These words (Hebrews 13:8) were written, in a time of rapid change, to readers who were trying to guard themselves against 'future shock' by retreating into their shell and staying there. Not that there was anything static about this unchanging Christ: that was largely their trouble. He was calling his people to leave their positions of fancied security to follow him along paths which they had not previously trodden, to venture into unknown territory for his sake and claim it for him. But they could be sure of his presence and help wherever he might lead them: the enterprise was his and he was totally dependable.

It was with this encouragement that Christians of the first few generations of our era carried the gospel to practically all the parts of the world that they knew. Time and again since those days a similar call has come when a new advance must be made into the unknown and unfamiliar, to occupy fresh areas of human life and endeavour under Jesus' leadership. To stand still is to fall behind him:

> New occasions teach new duties;
> Time makes ancient good uncouth:
> They must upward still and onward
> Who would keep abreast of truth.

But, as the author of those lines (James Russell Lowell) knew very well, the 'truth' to which they refer is embodied in Jesus.

'Truth unchanged, unchanging' is ever moving forward to the completion of God's purpose, and that purpose is being fulfilled, and will be consummated, in the immutable Jesus.

So he remains today: the crucified and risen one, Son of God and Son of Man, Saviour of the world and judge of the world, friend of sinners and Lord of all, present now and yet to come, Jesus Christ the same.

Notes to Text

Introduction

1. C. J. Cadoux, *The Life of Jesus* (West Drayton: Penguin Books, 1948), p. 10.
2. A. Schweitzer, *The Quest of the Historical Jesus* (London: A. & C. Black, 1910).
3. Cf. J. M. Robinson, *A New Quest of the Historical Jesus* (London: SCM Press, 1959); L. E. Keck, *A Future for the Historical Jesus* (London: SCM Press, 1972).
4. W. E. H. Lecky, *A History of European Morals from Augustus to Charlemagne*, II (London: Longmans Green & Co., ^{2}1869), p. 88.
5. Some of the material in this book has appeared in a series of twelve articles on 'The Jesus of History and the Christ of Faith' in *Harvester* (1984) and in a series of five entitled 'Who is Jesus?' in *Release Nationwide* (1984–85). Their substance is incorporated in the following chapters with the good will of the editors, to whom I express my gratitude.

Chapter 1

1. S. Radhakrishnan, *The Recovery of Faith* (London: Allen & Unwin, 1956), p. 159.
2. E. Brunner, *The Word and the World* (London: SCM, 1931), pp. 87, 88.
3. R. Bultmann, *Faith and Understanding*, I (London: SCM, 1969),

p. 241 (the rendering from the German original there is slightly different from that given here).
4. Cf. P. S. Minear, 'The Influences of Ecumenical Developments on New Testament Teaching', *Journal of Ecumenical Studies* 8 (1971), p. 287.
5. Hebrews 2:14–18; 4:14–16.
6. R. C. Moberly, 'The Incarnation as the Basis of Dogma', in C. Gore (ed.), *Lux Mundi* (London: John Murray, 1889), p. 243.

Chapter 2

1. Even when the positively Christian symbols AD (Year of our Lord) and BC (Before Christ) are replaced by the non-committal CE (Common Era) and BCE (Before the Common Era), the fact remains that the reckoning of the years runs forward and backward from the date of Jesus' birth, as calculated (not so accurately as might have been wished) by Dionysius Exiguus early in the sixth century.
2. They are discussed in my *Jesus and Christian Origins Outside the New Testament* (London: Hodder & Stoughton, [2]1984).
3. Our principal informant about Jewish history at the beginning of the Christian era is the Jewish historian Josephus (AD 37–*c.*100). An incomparable modern work on the subject is E. Schürer, *The History of the Jewish People in the Age of Jesus Christ*, revised and edited by G. Vermes and F. Millar, 3 volumes (Edinburgh: T. & T. Clark, 1973–   ). See also G. Vermes, *Jesus the Jew* (London: Collins, 1973), and *Jesus and the World of Judaism* (London: SCM, 1983).
4. See J. W. Drane, *Jesus and the Four Gospels* (Tring: Lion, 1979).
5. C. H. Dodd, *About the Gospels* (Cambridge: Cambridge University Press, 1950), p. 2.
6. Each of the five discourses is followed by the transitional formula, 'When Jesus had finished these sayings', or words to the same effect (Matthew 7:28; 11:1; 13:53; 19:1; 26:1).
7. See pp. 164–7.
8. On the Qumran texts see pp. 141–6; also my *Second Thoughts on the Dead Sea Scrolls* (Exeter: Paternoster, [3]1966) and *Jesus and Christian Origins*, pp. 66–81; on

the Nag Hammadi texts, *Jesus and Christian Origins*, pp. 110–156.
9. H. I. Bell and T. C. Skeat (eds), *Fragments of an Unknown Gospel and Other Early Christian Papyri* (London: British Museum, 1935); cf. *Jesus and Christian Origins*, pp. 160–164.
10. The catalogue reference is Mar Saba MS 65. The Greek text is translated and discussed in my Ethel Mary Wood lecture, *The 'Secret' Gospel of Mark* (London: Athlone Press, 1974).

Chapter 3

1. See pp. 141–6.
2. See pp. 129–34.
3. See pp. 128, 129.
4. Archelaus is mentioned in Matthew 2:22; Herod Antipas and Philip together in Luke 3:1; Herod Antipas by himself several times in the synoptic Gospels.
5. See Acts 1:14.
6. This phrase appears in Mark 7:3.
7. Josephus, *Jewish War*, 2.55–75; *Jewish Antiquities*, 17.269–295.
8. Josephus, *Jewish War*, 2.117, 118; *Jewish Antiquities*, 18.1–10. See pp. 135, 136.

Chapter 4

1. See Luke 7:36–50.
2. Luke 18:9–14.
3. Luke 15:11–32.
4. Luke 10:29–37.
5. Luke 22:37; Mark 10:45 (see p. 62).

Chapter 5

1. Matthew 21:32; Luke 11:1.
2. This was the encomium pronounced by Yohanan ben Zakkai (*c.* AD 30–100) on his pupil Eliezer ben Hyrcanus (*Ethics of the Fathers*, 2.8). He would have done better to teach Eliezer to think for himself, as he himself was conspicuously able to do.

Eliezer later showed himself so intransigent, so incapable of adapting his mind to changing conditions, that he had to be excommunicated.
3. Mark 7:14–23.
4. Matthew 10:1–15; Mark 6:7–13; Luke 9:1–6.
5. See p. 39.
6. Josephus, *Jewish War*, 2.125.
7. See H. W. Montefiore, *Jesus Across the Centuries* (London: SCM Press, 1983), pp. 53–66.

Chapter 6

1. See p. 64.
2. See *The Hard Sayings of Jesus*, pp. 92, 93.
3. See *Hard Sayings*, pp. 159, 160.
4. See *Hard Sayings*, pp. 26–28.
5. See *Hard Sayings*, pp. 32–34.
6. See pp. 100–2.
7. See pp. 112, 113.

Chapter 7

1. A phrase used in the interpretation of the parable of the tares: 'the good seed means the children of the kingdom' (Matthew 13:38).
2. Matthew 5:21,22 and 27,28.
3. Most notably in A. Schweitzer, *The Quest of the Historical Jesus* (London: A. & C. Black, 1910); also *The Mystery of the Kingdom of God* (London: A. & C. Black, 1925).
4. The two commandments (or the gist of them) are similarly linked in *The Testaments of the Twelve Patriarchs*, a work of approximately the same period as the New Testament (*Testament of Dan*, 5.3; *Testament of Issachar*, 5.2).
5. See p. 36.
6. J. Denney in W. R. Nicoll (ed.), *Letters of Principal James Denney to W. Robertson Nicoll* (London: Hodder & Stoughton, 1920), p. 71.
7. Jerusalem Targum I on Leviticus 22:28.
8. See p. 62.

Chapter 8

1. See p. 33.
2. See pp. 73, 74.
3. Luke 13:31–33.
4. Mark 11:27–33.
5. See pp. 39, 135–40.
6. As Jesus implied when, referring to money as 'mammon', he treated it as a rival to God: 'You cannot serve God and mammon' (Matthew 6:24; Luke 16:13).

Chapter 9

1. See Mark 6:52 for the disciples' lack of comprehension and John 6:26–65 for the discourse on the bread of life.
2. Mark 14:3–9; John 12:2–8.
3. Another view is that Judas was 'a zealot of the right' who 'betrayed Jesus to the Government because he honestly believed that Jesus intended to destroy the Temple' (J. A. Findlay, 'Why did Jesus tell his disciples to buy swords?' *British Weekly*, March 16, 1950).
4. Jesus may have deliberately dispensed with the lamb; see C. F. D. Moule, *The Birth of the New Testament* (London: A. & C. Black, [3]1981), pp. 22, 23.
5. See *The Hard Sayings of Jesus*, pp. 21–25.
6. The incident, recorded in Genesis 22:1–14, is referred to in Jewish tradition as the 'binding of Isaac' (cf. Genesis 22:9).

Chapter 10

1. See *Jesus and Christian Origins Outside the New Testament*, pp. 56, 57.
2. G. Vermes, *Jesus and the World of Judaism* (London: SCM, 1983), pp. viii, ix.
3. Compare Pilate's proposal with regard to Jesus in Luke 23:16: 'I will therefore chastise him and release him.'
4. Origen, *Commentary on Matthew*, 14.7.
5. On Annas see p. 37.
6. Coponius, the first Roman prefect of Judaea, had this preroga-

tive reserved to himself at his appointment in AD 6, according to Josephus (*Jewish War*, 2.117); see also John 18:31.
7. C. H. Dodd, *About the Gospels* (Cambridge: Cambridge University Press, 1950), pp. 37f.
8. Mark 15:6–11; John 18:39,40.

Chapter 11

1. See, for these arguments, P. Benoit, 'Praetorium, Lithostroton and Gabbatha', in *Jesus and the Gospel*, I (New York: Herder, 1973), pp. 167–188.
2. N. H. Snaith, *The Jews from Cyrus to Herod* (Wallington: Religious Education Press, 1949), p. 48. The incident is recorded by Josephus, *Jewish War*, 1.97; *Antiquities*, 13.380.
3. See pp. 38–9.
4. A full account of this discovery, from various expert angles (archaeological and anthropological) was given in the *Israel Exploration Journal* 20 (1970), pp. 18–59, by V. Tzaferis, J. Naveh and N. Haas.
5. When one of the psalmists said, 'for me it is good to be near God' (Psalm 73:28), it was evidently nearness in heart and not a ritual approach that he had in mind.
6. See further pp. 156, 157 below. (In Luke 23:47 the centurion's words are rendered: 'Certainly this man was innocent!')
7. On the subject of this chapter the reader is urged to study Michael Green's volume in this series: *The Empty Cross of Jesus* (London: Hodder & Stoughton, 1984).

Chapter 12

1. John 19:31–37.
2. See pp. 110, 111.
3. Matthew 28:11–15.
4. D. L. Sayers, *The Man Born to be King* (London: Gollancz, 1943), p. 33.
5. M. D. Goulder, 'Jesus, the Man of Universal Destiny', in J. Hick (ed.), *The Myth of God Incarnate* (London: SCM, 1977), p. 59.
6. B. Lindars, 'Christ and Salvation', *Bulletin of the John Rylands University Library of Manchester* 64 (1981–82), p. 493.

7. C. S. Lewis, *Miracles* (London: Bles, 1947), pp. 148–169.
8. C. H. Dodd, 'The Appearances of the Risen Christ', in *More New Testament Studies* (Manchester: Manchester University Press, 1968), p. 115.
9. Celsus, *True Word*, quoted by Origen, *Against Celsus*, 2.55.
10. See C. F. D. Moule, 'The Post-Resurrection Appearances in the Light of Festival Pilgrimages', *New Testament Studies* 4 (1957–58), pp. 58–61.

Chapter 13

1. See p. 34.
2. See p. 79.
3. So, for example, Paul Winter, *On the Trial of Jesus* (Berlin: de Gruyter, 1961), p. 120: 'Jesus himself in his teaching stood closer to early Pharisaism than to any other school of thought.'
4. It was not uncommon for Jews of the dispersion (and even Palestinian Jews) to have both a Jewish and a Gentile name: Saul was his Jewish name, Paul his Roman name.
5. Palestinian Talmud, tractate *Berakot* 9.7.
6. See John 3:1–15; 7:50–52 (also 19:39).
7. See p. 39, 51, 84.
8. See Numbers 25:10–13; 1 Kings 19:10; 1 Maccabees 2:24–26.
9. See p. 85.
10. See pp. 51, 52.
11. The Babylonian Talmud once refers to the insurgents in Jerusalem as *biryonim* (tractate *Gittin* 56a).
12. S. G. F. Brandon, *Jesus and the Zealots* (Manchester: Manchester University Press, 1967), p. 16. But see my *Hard Sayings*, pp. 240–242.
13. See Brandon, *Jesus and the Zealots*, pp. 221–282.
14. See my *Second Thoughts on the Dead Sea Scrolls* (Exeter: Paternoster, [3]1966).
15. See Luke 2:25; 23:50,51.
16. From May 1948 until the Six Days War (June 1967), Qumran belonged to the Hashemite Kingdom of Jordan.
17. G. Lankester Harding, in *Illustrated London News*, September 3, 1955.
18. E. Wilson, *The Scrolls from the Dead Sea* (London: W. H. Allen, 1955), p. 129.

19. A. Dupont-Sommer, *The Dead Sea Scrolls* (Oxford: Blackwell, 1952), p. 99. (The wording of the quotation here is an independent rendering of the French original.)
20. J. L. Teicher, 'The Dead Sea Scrolls – Documents of the Jewish-Christian Sect of Ebionites', *Journal of Jewish Studies* 2 (1950–51), pp. 67–99.
21. B. E. Thiering, *Redating the Teacher of Righteousness* (Sydney, N.S.W.: Theological Explorations, 1979); *The Gospels and Qumran* (Sydney, N.S.W.: Theological Explorations, 1981); *The Qumran Origins of the Christian Church* (Sydney, N.S.W.: Theological Explorations, 1983).

Chapter 14

1. Philippians 2:6–11. See pp. 201, 202.
2. G. Lyttelton, *Observations on the Conversion and Apostleship of St Paul* (London: R. Dodsley, 1747), preface.
3. John Masefield, *The Everlasting Mercy*.
4. See M. Green, *I Believe in the Holy Spirit* (London: Hodder & Stoughton, 1975).

Chapter 15

1. This subject is treated more fully in F. F. Bruce, *The Spreading Flame* (Exeter: Paternoster, 1982), pp. 302–308.
2. See pp. 22, 209.
3. See p. 111.
4. See my *Jesus and Christian Origins Outside the New Testament* (London: Hodder & Stoughton, [2]1984), pp. 172f.
5. See *Jesus and Christian Origins*, pp. 170, 175.
6. See pp. 164–70.
7. See *The Spreading Flame*, pp. 241f., 253–260.
8. Luke 6:36 (see p. 75).
9. See *The Spreading Flame*, pp. 305f.
10. *The Human Face of God* is the title of J. A. T. Robinson's Hulsean Lectures on Christology (London: SCM Press, 1973). The idea of God's human face goes back to Ezekiel 1:26 (see p. 172).
11. Augustine, *Sermons* 121.5. (Here, as usual in the writings of the

Christian Fathers, the designation 'the Son of Man' has lost most of the distinctive force which it has in the Gospels and refers simply to Jesus as a human being.)

Chapter 16

1. See pp. 147, 148, 201, 202.
2. See R. H. Gundry, 'The Form, Meaning and Background of the Hymn quoted in 1 Timothy 3:16', in W. W. Gasque and R. P. Martin (eds), *Apostolic History and the Gospel* (Exeter: Paternoster, 1970), pp. 203–222.

Chapter 17

1. See *The Hard Sayings of Jesus*, pp. 104–106.
2. See *Hard Sayings*, pp. 110, 111.
3. Jesus' known attitude to tax-collectors might warn one against supposing that these words express a totally negative attitude to Gentiles.
4. G. Vermes, *Jesus and the World of Judaism* (London: SCM Press, 1983), pp. 54f.
5. An attempt is made to expound these texts more fully in F. F. Bruce, *The Gospel of John* (Basingstoke: Pickering & Inglis, 1983).

Chapter 18

1. This interrogation occurs in John 1:19–23.
2. See F. F. Bruce, *Second Thoughts on the Dead Sea Scrolls* (Exeter: Paternoster, [3]1966), pp. 80–91.
3. Hebrews 1:9.
4. Deuteronomy 34:10.
5. Revelation 1:8,17,18; 22:13.
6. In experience, indeed, it is impossible to distinguish between the realisation of Jesus' presence through the Spirit and its realisation in any other way.
7. Alfred, Lord Tennyson, *Locksley Hall*.
8. Daniel 7:13,14; see pp. 64, 101.

9. J. H. Newman, 'Waiting for Christ', *Parochial and Plain Sermons*, vi (London: Longmans, 1896), p. 241.
10. On the subject of this chapter see S. H. Travis, *Christian Hope and the Future of Man* (Leicester: Inter-Varsity Press, 1980); *I Believe in the Second Coming of Jesus* (London: Hodder & Stoughton, 1982).

Chapter 19

1. *Didache* (*Teaching of the Twelve Apostles*) 10:6.
2. See pp. 147, 148, 164.
3. I have discussed this Christ-hymn more fully in my *Philippians*, Good News Bible Commentary (San Francisco: Harper & Row, 1983/Basingstoke: Pickering & Inglis, 1984), pp. 44–55.
4. Moreover, in the Greek version (unlike the Hebrew original) there is a change of speaker at this point. Hitherto the psalmist has been voicing his plea to God; from now on God answers him, and the writer to the Hebrews might well ask who it was that could be addressed as 'Lord' by God – and draw what in his eyes would be the only possible conclusion.

For Further Reading

ANDERSON, N., *The Teaching of Jesus*. The Jesus Library (London: Hodder & Stoughton, 1983).

ANDERSON, N., *Jesus Christ: The Witness of History* (Leicester: Inter-Varsity Press, 1985).

BAMMEL, E., and MOULE, C. F. D. (eds), *Jesus and the Politics of His Day* (Cambridge: Cambridge University Press, 1984).

BETZ, O., *What do we know about Jesus?* (London: SCM Press, 1968).

BORNKAMM, G., *Jesus of Nazareth* (London: Hodder & Stoughton, 1960).

BRUCE, F. F., *The Hard Sayings of Jesus*. The Jesus Library (London: Hodder & Stoughton, 1983).

BRUCE, F. F., *Jesus and Christian Origins Outside the New Testament* (London: Hodder & Stoughton, 1984).

BRUCE, F. F., *The Work of Jesus* (Eastbourne: Kingsway Publications, 1984).

DAHL, N. A., *The Crucified Messiah and Other Essays* (Minneapolis: Augsburg Press, 1974).

DODD, C. H., *The Founder of Christianity* (London: Collins, 1971).

DRANE, J. W., *Jesus and the Four Gospels* (Tring: Lion Publishing, 1979).

FRANCE, R. T., *The Man They Crucified: A Portrait of Jesus* (London: Inter-Varsity Press, 1975).

GRANT, M., *Jesus: A Historian's Review of the Gospels* (London: Weidenfeld & Nicolson, 1977).

GREEN, M., *The Empty Cross of Jesus*. The Jesus Library (London: Hodder & Stoughton, 1984).

GREEN, M., *Jesus Spells Freedom* (London: Inter-Varsity Press, 1972).

GROLLENBERG, L., *Jesus* (London: SCM Press, 1978).

GUTHRIE, D., *A Shorter Life of Jesus* (Grand Rapids: Zondervan, 1970).

HARVEY, A. E., *Jesus and the Constraints of History* (London: Duckworth, 1982).

HENGEL, M., *The Atonement* (London: SCM Press, 1981).

HENGEL, M., *Crucifixion* (London: SCM Press, 1977).

HENGEL, M., *The Son of God* (London: SCM Press, 1976).

HENGEL, M., *Victory over Violence* (London: SPCK, 1975).

HENGEL, M., *Was Jesus a Revolutionist?* (Philadelphia: Fortress Press, 1971).

KÄSEMANN, E., *Jesus Means Freedom* (London: SCM Press, 1969).

MANSON, T. W., *The Servant-Messiah* (Cambridge: Cambridge University Press, 1953; reprinted, Grand Rapids: Baker, 1977).

MARSHALL, I. H., *I Believe in the Historical Jesus* (London: Hodder & Stoughton, 1977).

MARSHALL, I. H., *The Origins of New Testament Christology* (Leicester: Inter-Varsity Press, 1976).

MARSHALL, I. H., *The Work of Christ* (Exeter: Paternoster Press, 1969).

MEYE, R. P., *Jesus and the Twelve Disciples* (Grand Rapids: Eerdmans, 1968).

MITTON, C. L., *Jesus: The Fact Behind the Faith* (London: Mowbrays 1973/Grand Rapids: Eerdmans, 1974).

MOULE, C. F. D., *The Origin of Christology* (Cambridge: Cambridge University Press, 1977).

NEIL, W., *The Life and Teaching of Jesus* (London: Hodder & Stoughton, 1965).

NEILL, S., *The Supremacy of Jesus*. The Jesus Library (London: Hodder & Stoughton, 1984).

PETER, J. F., *Finding the Historical Jesus* (London: Collins, 1965).

PHILLIPS, J. B., *Ring of Truth* (London: Hodder & Stoughton, 1967).

SCHWEIZER, E., *Jesus* (London: SCM Press, 1971).

TROCMÉ, É., *Jesus and His Contemporaries* (London: SCM Press, 1973).

VERMES, G., *Jesus the Jew* (London: Collins, 1973).

ZAHRNT, H., *The Historical Jesus* (London: Collins, 1963).

Index of
Biblical References

Index of Authors

THE JESUS LIBRARY
Michael Green, series editor

Jesus: Lord & Savior

F. F. Bruce